THE WISE WORLD OF ENGLISH PROVERBS

SC Gupta
Kumkum Gupta

Arihant Publications (I) Pvt Ltd, Meerut

ॐ © Author

Delhi Office: 4577/15, Ramchhaya, Agarwal Road, Darya Ganj, New Delhi - 2
Phone : 011-23280316, 47630600 ; Fax : 011-43540876

Head Office : Kalindi, TP Nagar, Meerut, Phone : 0121-2401479, 2512970, 2402029 ;
Fax : 0121-2401648, Email : info@arihantbooks.com

ॐ **Zonal & Regional Offices :**

North Zone — **Agra**: 8/195, New Engineers' Colony, Kaushalpur, Agra, Ph. 0562 – 6451531, Email: arihant_agra02@yahoo.co.in; **Delhi–1 (for Delhi & NCR) :** 4577/15, Ramchhaya, Agarwal Road, Darya Ganj, New Delhi – 110002, Ph. 011 – 23280316, Fax. 011 – 43540876, Email: arihant_delhi07@yahoo.co.in; **Delhi–2 (for Haryana, Himachal, J&K & Punjab) :** 4577/15, Ramchhaya, Agarwal Road, Darya Ganj, New Delhi – 110002, Ph. 011 – 23280316, Fax. 011 – 43540876, Email: arihant_delhi07@yahoo.co.in **Jaipur**: C–8, Link Road, Jalupura MD Road, Near Hotel Apoorva, Jaipur – 302 001 (Raj), Ph. 0141 – 4033077, Email : deepmahur85@gmail.com; **Kota**: 5-J-18, Talwardi, Behind T.T. Hospital, Kota–324009 (Rajasthan.), 0744–2406760, Email : arihant_kota@yahoo.co.in; **Lucknow**: C – 22,Vijay Laxmi Transport Building, Transport Nagar, Kanpur Road, Lucknow – 226 012 (UP), Ph. 0522 – 6459009, Fax : 0522-4028575, Email : arihant_lko@yahoo.com; **Haldwani**: Raja Enterprises, Varun Complex, Rampur Road, Haldwani (Uttrakhand), Ph. 05946 – 235456 ; Email : arihant_kashipur@yahoo.co.in; **Meerut**: Kalindi, TP Nagar, Meerut, Ph: 0121-6534323, Email: arihant_meerutbranch@yahoo.co.in.

East Zone — **Bhubaneshwar**: 14, Shahid Nagar, Bhubaneshwar – 751007 (Orissa), Ph. 064 – 2503050, 09938211103, Email : bhubaneshwar@arihantbooks.com; **Kolkata**: 4, Tottee Lane, Kolkata – 700016 (WB), Ph. 033 – 22526713, Fax. 033 – 22523564, Email: arihant_kol@yahoo.co.in; **Guwahati**: Aastha Towers, Ist Floor, Module No. XIII, CK Road, Pan Bazar, Guwahati – 781 001, (Asom) Ph. 0361 – 2731599, E-mail : arihant_guwahati@yahoo.co.in; **Patna**: Gangotri Complex, U/465, Lohia Nagar, Kankarbagh, Patna – 20 (Bihar), Ph. 0612 – 2360623, Email: cafpatna@rediffmail.com.

Central Zone — **Nagpur**: 27, Nathuji Pise Complex, Opp. Mokshadham, New Gate, Beside Hanuman Mandir, Great Nag Road, Nagpur – 14, (Maharashtra), Ph. 0712 – 2748211 ; Email : arihant_nagpur1@yahoo.co.in.

South Zone — **Hyderabad**: Plot No.–115, SBI Colony, Kavadiguda, Near Sri Satya Sai Temple, Hyderabad–500020, Ph. 040 – 65347774, 66107772, Email: hyd.arihant@gmail.com; **Bengaluru**: 362, 10th Main, 2nd Cross, Ist Block, Basaveshwara Nagar, Bengaluru-560079, Mob : +919242693192

ॐ No part of this publication may be reproduced, stored in a retrieval system or distributed in any form or by any means, electronic, mechanical, photocopying, recording, scanning or otherwise without the prior written permission of the publishers. Arihant publications have acquired the information contained in this book from the sources believed to be reliable. However, Arihant publications or its authors or the editors don't take any responsibility for the absolute accuracy of the information published and the damages suffered due to the use of this information.

All disputes are subject to Meerut (UP) jurisdiction only.

ॐ **Laser Typesetting** : Arihant DTP Unit, Meerut

For further information on
Arihant Group, visit log in : www.arihantbooks.com

Preface

Knowledge of proverbs is necessary for perfect knowledge of a language. In the form of short, easily memorable phrases, the proverbs contain a great treasure of folk wisdom; and through use of a short proverb, it's often easier to express an idea better and more convincingly, than with a long speech. English language learners, often struggling with a limited vocabulary, find these memorable proverbs easy to learn and fun to use. Using the right proverb at the right moment gives students a tremendous sense of competency and fluency in English.

This book, 'A collection of Popular & Interesting Proverbs' is a treasure trove for the students keen to enrich their English language skill. The book starts with all the interesting information on proverbs, followed by a meticulous collection of traditional proverbs, proverbs from different countries, conflicting proverbs, etc. What makes the book more worth to its reader is the incorporation of quotable quotes from great personalities of all times.

Honest & meticulous efforts have been taken in developing the content of the book, but there is always a scope for improvement. We invite and welcome any feedback & suggestions for the improvement of this book in subsequent editions.

SC Gupta
Kumkum Gupta

Contents

A Unique World of Interesting Proverbs

What are Proverbs?

Proverbs are wise sayings. They are usually short, to the point, memorable and popular. They are advisory and eye openers by nature. The proverbs contains simple truths from experience over the years. Most of the proverbs exhibit simple rhyme and elegant balance.

Are Proverbs Different From Idioms?

Idioms, like Proverbs, are common sayings. Idioms usually do not offer any advice. For example, to blow one's own trumpet, which means to praise oneself is an idiom. It may be converted into a proverbial expression: Don't blow your own trumpet. There is no clear dividing line between idiomatic phrases and proverbial expressions. When an idiomatic phrase becomes widely popular, it is regarded a proverb.

Where do Proverbs Originate From?

Proverbs usually originate from two primary sources—the common men and the wise people. Something commonly experienced is documented by the wise, and something written by the wise is liked and frequently used by the common man.

Many English proverbs also owe their origin to the Bible :

A soft answer turneth away wrath

Something is better than nothing

In addition to the Bible, several proverbs are believed to have their origin in the works of William Shakespeare and other great authors. It is difficult to be certain whether these proverbs were truly invented by Shakespeare or other authors or were already in existence, before or around his time. For example :

➤ Brevity is the soul of wit
   (from Hamlet)

- Cowards die many times before their deaths
  (*from Julius Caesar*)

- Laugh and the world laughs with you, weep and you weep alone
  (*from the poem Solitude by Ella Wheeler Wilcox*)

- A little learning is a dangerous thing
  (*from Essay on Criticism by Alexander Pope*)

- A thing of beauty is a joy for ever
  (*from the poem Endymion by John Keats*)

How are Proverbs to be Interpreted?

Proverbs contain popular wisdom acquired by mankind over the ages. Proverbs are to be interpreted primarily in two ways – literally and metaphorically.

Many Proverbs contain a universal truth and are to be interpreted literally. For example,

- Hope for the best and prepare for the worst

- One is never too old to learn

Examples of Proverbs that apply to a host of situations and are to be interpreted in a broad metaphorical sense (not just literally) are :

- A bird in the hand is worth two in the bush

- Between two stools you fall to the ground

What is the Role of Proverbs in Learning and Education?

Learning, interpreting and understanding the entire gamut of Proverbs allows an individual to formulate a philosophy of life. Proverbs offer learning for all ages whether old, young; men or women. Proverbs determine actions and emotions of an individual. Proverbs are actually the experience and truth felt by wise and common men, guide the mankind in times of difficulty, and when there is double crossing in the path to lead.

Traditional Proverbs

A

- An apple a day keeps the doctor away

- A bad workman always blames his tools
  (To blame the tools for bad workmanship is an attempt to excuse one's lack of skill.)

- A bird in the hand is worth two in the bush
  (What you have is worth more than what you dream about.)

- A burnt child dreads the fire
  (A bad experience or a horrifying incident may scar one's attitude or thinking for a lifetime.)

- A cat may look at a king
  (If a cat may look at the king, then I have a right to look where I please.)

- A chain is no stronger than its weakest link
  (The strength of any group depends on the individual strength of each of its members.)

- A closed mouth catches no flies
  (It is often safer to keep one's mouth shut.)

- A coward dies a thousand times before his death. The valiant never taste of death but once
  [A coward constantly and fearfully imagines his own demise, while the valiant give no thought to how they might be harmed. Also: worrying about a forthcoming disaster may cause as much (or even more) pain as the disaster when it occurs (but does neither change it nor make it easier).]

- A fool and his money are soon parted

- A fox smells its own lair first and A fox smells its own stink first
  (The fault one notices in another is often a fault of the first person.)

- A friend in need is a friend indeed
  (A friend who helps when one is in trouble is a real friend.)

- A friend of all is a friend to none
  (One can't be a friend of all, if any one pretends so, he is not a friend of anybody.)

- A good beginning makes a good ending

- A good man in an evil society seems the greatest villain of all

- A good surgeon has an eagle's eye, a lion's heart, and a lady's hand

- A great talker is a great liar
  (*A smooth and persuasive talker may be a good liar.*)

- A guilty conscience needs no accuser

- A hungry man is an angry man
  (*A person, who does not get what he wants or needs, is a frustrated person and will be easily provoked to rage.*)

- A kite rises against the wind

- A lie can be halfway around the world before the truth gets its boots on
  (*A great lie may be widely accepted before the truth comes to light. *)

- A little knowledge is a dangerous thing

- A loaded wagon makes no noise
  (*People with real worth don't talk about it.*)

- A miss by an inch is a miss by a mile
  (*A miss is as good as a mile.*)

- A man is as old as he feels
  (*A person's age is immaterial. It is only when he thinks and feels that he is ageing, that he actually becomes old.*)

- A paragraph should be like a lady's skirt—long enough to cover the essentials but short enough to keep it interesting

- A penny saved is a penny earned
  (*By being thrifty, one will be able to save up.*)

- A man is known by the company he keeps

- A picture is worth a thousand words

- A pot of milk is ruined by a drop of poison

- A rolling stone gathers no moss
  (*A person who never settles in one place or who often changes his job will not succeed in life; one who is always changing his mind will never get anything done.*)

- A stitch in time saves nine
  (*Fix the small problem now before it becomes larger and harder to fix.*)

- A whistling woman and a crowing hen are neither fit for God nor man
- Absence makes the heart grow fonder
  (One usually desires another more when he or she is far away.)
- Actions speak louder than words
  (Children usually learn more from the examples set by their elders than from what they are told; a person's character is judged by the things he does and not by what he says.)
- Advice most needed is least heeded
- After dinner, sit a while; after supper, walk a mile
- All cats love fish but hate to get their paws wet
- All flowers are not in one garland
- All frills and no knickers
  (All style and no substance.)
- All good things come to an end
- All hat and no cattle
  (All talk and appearance and little or no substance.)
- All roads lead to Rome
- All's fair in love and war
- All for one and one for all
- All's well that ends well
- All sizzle and no steak
  (All style and no substance.)
- All that glitters is not gold
  (Do not be deceived by things or offers that appear to be attractive.)
- All things come to him who waits
- All work and no play makes Jack a dull boy
- All play and no work makes Jack a mere toy
- A man's home is his castle
- A person is king in his home
- An eye for an eye and a tooth for a tooth
  (Retribution should be equitable, proportionate and "fit the crime". Biblical reference, modern usage often connotes support for capital punishment.)

- An ounce of prevention is worth a pound of cure
  (Similar to that of A stitch in time saves nine. Preventing something in advance is better than fixing it later on.)
- An idle brain is the devil's workshop
  (One who has nothing to do will be tempted to do many mischievous acts.)
- An ounce of discretion is worth a pound of wit
  (It is better to be careful and discrete than to be clever.)
- Any time means no time
  (When an event is not decided on or planned earlier, it will never take place.)
- A picture is worth a thousand words
- April showers bring May flowers
- Ask me no questions, I'll tell you no lies
  (Ask no questions and hear no lies.)
- As fit as a fiddle
  (Quite fit and well.)
- As you make your bed, so you must lie in it
- A Smack in the mouth often offends
  (Meaning you will offend the proprieter should you ask for credit. Pay for your goods!)
- As you sow, so you shall reap
  (One will either enjoy or suffer the consequences of his earlier actions or inactions.)
- A watched kettle never boils
  (Worrying over something can make the task seem to take longer than it should.)
- A woman's work is never done
  (Meaning that a man's traditional role as breadwinner may keep him occupied from sun-up to sun-down, but the traditional roles of a woman demand even longer hours of work.)
- A word spoken is past recalling
  (What's done is done.)

B

- Barking dogs seldom bite
  (Those who make loud threats seldom carry them out. Also - People, who are busy complaining, rarely take more concrete hostile action.)

- Be careful what you wish for, you might just get it
  (Things greatly desired have unintended consequences.)

- Beauty is in the eye of the beholder
  (The idea of beauty is personal.)

- Beauty is only skin deep, but ugliness goes straight to the bone

- Beauty may open doors but only virtue enters

- Before criticizing a man, walk a mile in his shoes
  (One should not criticize a person without understanding their situation.)

- Beggars can't be choosers
  (Those who are in need of help, should not criticize the help, they receive.)

- Behind every good man is a woman

- Better to have it and not need it than to need it and not have it

- Better to remain silent and be thought a fool, than to open your mouth and remove all doubt
  (It is better to remain silent and thought a fool, than to speak and remove all doubt about that you are really a fool.)

- Better late than never
  (To do something that is right, profitable, or good a little late is still better than not doing it at all.)

- Better safe than sorry
  (It is better to take precautions when it's possible that something can go amiss than to regret doing nothing later if something should indeed go wrong.)

- Beware of the Bear when he tucks in his shirt

- Between the devil and the deep sea
  (To choose between two equally bad alternatives in a serious dilemma.)

- Birds of a feather flock together
  (People of the same sort of character or belief always go together.)

- Beware of the false prophets, who come to you in sheep's clothing, and inwardly are ravening wolves (*Mathew; bible quote*)
- Beware of Greeks bearing gifts
- Bitter pills may have blessed effects
- Blood is thicker than water
  (*Bonds between family members are stronger than other relationships.*)
- Blood will out
  (*A person's ancestry or upbringing will eventually show.*)
- Bloom where you are planted
- Boys will be boys
  (*Boys are traditionally expected to misbehave, while girls are not.*)
- Brain is better than brawn
- Bread is the staff of life

- Call a spade a spade
  (*If you say that someone calls a spade a spade, you mean that they speak frankly and directly, often about embarrassing or unpleasant subjects; an informal expression.*)
- Charity begins at home
  (*A person's first obligation should be to help the member of his own family before he can begin thinking of talking about helping others.*)
- Chance favours the prepared mind
- Cobbler, stick to thy last
  (*Tend to what you know.*)
- Common sense ain't common
- Curiosity killed the cat
- Cut your coat according to your cloth
- Cry me a river, build a bridge and get over it
- Damned if you do, damned if you don't
  (*Refers to a situation where both possibilities will lead to harm.*)

- Dead men tell no lies
  (Often used as an argument for killing someone whose knowledge of a secret may cause one loss or get into serious trouble.)

- Desperate times call for desperate measures

- Discretion is the better part of valour
  (If you say discretion is the better part of valour, you mean that avoiding a dangerous or unpleasant situation is sometimes the most sensible thing to do.)

- Different strokes for different folks
  (Different people have different preferences.)

- Do unto others as you would have done to you

- Doctors make the worst patients

- Don't bite the hand that feeds you
  (Behave deferentially to those who provide for you.)

- Don't burn your bridges before they're crossed
  (Do not act in such a way as to leave yourself no alternatives.)

- Don't count your chickens before they're hatched

- Don't cry over spilt milk
  (Do not be excessively regretful of minor accidents.)

- Don't cross your bridges before you get to them

- Don't cut off your nose to spite your face
  (Do not act to spite someone else if it is damaging to yourself.)

- Don't eat yellow snow

- Don't fall before you're pushed

- Don't have too many irons in the fire
  (Do not take on more responsibility than you can handle at any one time.)

- Don't judge a book by its cover
  (Do not judge by appearances.)

- Don't look a gift horse in the mouth

- Do not look for faults in a gift
  (Looking at a horse's mouth is one classic way to judge its health.)

- Don't make a mountain out of a molehill
  (Don't exaggerate small things.)

- Don't mend what ain't broken
  (*If it ain't broke, don't fix it.*)
- Don't put all your eggs in one basket
  (*One should not risk everything he has in a single venture.*)
- Don't put the cart before the horse
  (*Do things in the correct order.*)
- Don't shut the barn door after the horse is gone
  (*Prepare for things to go wrong rather than worrying about them after the fact.*)
- Don't spit into the wind
- Don't take life too seriously; you'll never get out of it alive
- Don't throw out the baby with the bathwater
  (*Do not, in an attempt to remove something undesirable, lose things that are valuable.*)
- Don't cross a bridge before you come to it
  (*Don't fret unnecessarily about future problems.*)
- Doubt is the beginning, not the end, of wisdom

E

- Eat to live, but do not live to eat
  (*Man was created for a divine purpose and he has a destiny with his Creator - he was not born just to enjoy food.*)
- Early to bed and early to rise, makes a man healthy, wealthy and wise
- Empty vessels make the most noise
  (*Those people, who have a little knowledge, usually talk the most and make the greatest fuss.*)
- Ends justify the means
- Even a dog can distinguish between being stumbled over and being kicked
- Every dog has its day
  (*Everyone will get a period of success or satisfaction during his lifetime.*)
- Every cloud has a silver lining
  (*If you say that every cloud has a silver lining, you mean that every sad or unpleasant situation has a positive side to it. If you talk about silver lining you are talking about something positive that comes out of a sad or unpleasant situation.*)

- Everyone wants to go to heaven, but no one wants to die

- Every one can find fault, few can do better
  (*It is easier to find fault in other people's actions or methods than to do it properly or correctly.*)

- Even a broken/stopped clock is right twice a day
  (*Excuses are like butts, everybody has them and they all stink.*)

- The early bird catches the worm

F

- Faint heart never won fair lady
  (*To succeed in life, one must have the courage to pursue what he wants.*)

- Fair exchange is no robbery
  (*A contract is fair as long as both the parties understand and agree to the conditions willingly; after a deal is closed, neither side can turn around and say that he was unfairly treated.*)

- Familiarity breeds contempt
  (*Long experience of someone or something can make one so aware of the faults as to be scornful.*)

- Fine feathers make fine birds

- Fine words butter no parsnips
  (*Actions speak louder than words.*)

- Fire is a good servant but a bad master
  (*Fire, like any other manmade tool or device, will serve man well only when it is controlled and used wisely.*)

- First come, first served
  (*The first in line will be attended to first.*)

- First deserve, then desire

- First things first
  (*Do more important things before other things.*)

- Fool me once, shame on you. Fool me twice, shame on me

- Fools rush in where angels fear to tread

- Alexander Pope.

- For want of a nail, the horseshoe was lost
  (*For want of a nail, the horseshoe was lost; for want of a horseshoe, the horse was lost; for want of a horse, the rider was lost; for want of a rider, the battle was lost; for want of a battle, the kingdom was lost, and all for want of a nail.*)

➤ Fortune knocks once at every man's door
(Everyone gets at least one good opportunity in his lifetime; everyone has the opportunity to be successful in life.)

➤ Forewarned is forearmed

➤ Fretting cares make grey hairs

 **G**

➤ Give and take is fair play

➤ Give a dog a bad name and hang him

➤ Give a man a fish and you feed him for a day; teach a man to fish and you feed him for a lifetime

➤ Give, and ye shall receive *Jesus*

➤ Give the devil his due
(Be just and fair-minded, even to the one who does not deserve much or who is unfriendly or unfair; we should punish a person according to his wrongdoings.)

➤ Going the whole nine yards

➤ Going to Hell in a handbasket
(Something or a situation is quickly taking a turn for the worse without effort or with great haste.)

➤ God takes care of drunks

➤ God cures and the physician takes the fee

➤ God don't like ugly and he ain't stuck on pretty

➤ God helps those who help themselves
(God only helps those people who work hard and make an honest effort.)

➤ Good eating deserves good drinking

➤ Good fences make good neighbors

➤ Good men are hard to find

➤ Good poon needs no bush
(Something desirable of quality and substance need not be embellished. It was customary since early times to hang a grapevine, ivy or other greenery over the door of a tavern or way stop to advertise the availability of drink within. Once something establishes a good reputation for quality, the advertisement is rendered superfluous.)

➤ Good things come in small packages

- The grass is always greener on the other side of the fence
- Great haste makes great waste
  (If one does things hastily, he will make a lot of mistakes - he will need to spend a lot of time correcting those mistakes later.)
- Great minds think alike
  (Wise people will normally think and behave alike in certain situations.)
- Great talkers are little doers
  (Those people who talk a lot and are always teaching others, usually do not do much work.)
- Great oaks from little acorns grow
- Green leaves and brown leaves fall from the same tree
  (Things change over time.– If you are good at one aspect of a skill, you should be skilled at the other aspects, such as a painter who says he can't draw, yet both painting and drawing are aspects of art.– No matter of the outside, we are all the same inside.)
- Grow where you are planted
- Give respect, get respect

- Habit is second nature
  (An act done repeatedly and often enough will sooner or later become a habit or second nature.)
- Hair of the dog that bit you
- Half a loaf is better than none
  (Be thankful for what you've got.)
- Handsome is as handsome does
- Hang a thief when he's young, and he'll not steal when he's old
- Happy wife, happy life
- Hard cases make bad law
- Hard words break no bones
- Haste makes waste
- Have not, want not
- He, who dares, wins
- He who fails to prepare, prepares to fail

- Health is better than wealth
- Heaven hath no rage like love to hatred turned, nor Hell a fury like a woman scorned
- Heaven protects children, sailors and drunks
- Hell hath no fury like a woman scorned, which is merely a spark compared to the Sun as a measure of the power of God's wrath
- He who hesitates is lost
- He, who knows, does not speak. He, who speaks, does not know
- He laughs best who laughs last
  (*A person, who does his best, is the one who will get the greatest satisfaction in the end.*)
- He, who lives too fast, goes to his grave too soon
- He, who stands for nothing, will fall for everything
- He, who will steal an egg, will steal an ox
- He, who lives by the sword, shall die by the sword
- He, who pays the piper, calls the tune
  (*To be able to contol the details of a situation by virtue of being the one who bears the cost or provides for others.*)
- He who sleeps, forgets his hunger
- Hindsight is 20/20
  (*It is always easy to see your mistakes after they occur.*)
- His bark is worse than his bite
  (*He will talk about consequences more than act.*)
- History repeats itself   *Mark Twain*
- Home is where the heart is
- Honesty is the best policy
  (*Being honest is believed to be the best route to take.*)
- Honey catches more flies than vinegar
  (*One can get more cooperation from others by being nice.*)
- Hope for the best, expect the worst
  (*Pray for the best, prepare for the worst.*)
- Hope is life
- Hope springs eternal   *Alexander Pope*
- Hunger is the best spice

- It is better to die on one's feet than live on one's knees
- Idle minds are the devil's workshop
- If at first you don't succeed, try, try again
- If if's and but's were pots and pans, there would be no tinklers
- If it ain't broke, don't fix it
  (*If it isn't broken, don't fix it.*)
- If life gives you lemons, make lemonade.
- If something can go wrong, it will   *Murphy's Law*
- If the shoe fits, wear it
- If the mountain won't come to Muhammad, Muhammad must go to the mountain
  (*If one can't have one's way, one must give in. For example, **Since you can't come here for the holiday, I'll go to your house—if the mountain won't come to Muhammad, Muhammad must go to the mountain.** This expression is based on a tale that Muhammad once sought proof of his teachings by ordering a mountain to come to him. When it did not move, he maintained that God had been merciful, for if it had indeed moved, they all would have been crushed by it.*)
- If wishes were horses, beggars would ride
- If you buy quality, you only cry once
- If you buy cheaply, you pay dearly
- If you can't beat them, join them
- If you can't be good, be careful
- If you can't take the heat, get out of the kitchen
- If you catch the rabbit, you can fry the rabbit. Then put him in a stew
- If you don't buy a ticket, you can't win the raffle
- If you don't have anything nice to say, dont say anything at all!
- If you keep your mouth shut, you won't put your foot in it
- If you want a thing done right, do it yourself
- If you were born to be shot, you'll never be hung
- If you're in a hole, stop digging

- If you're not part of the solution, you're part of the problem
- Ignorance is bliss
- Improvement means deterioration   *Hutber's Law*
- In for a penny, in for a pound
- In order to get where you want to go, you first have to leave where you are
- In the land of the blind, the one-eyed man is king
- In the end, a man's motives are second to his accomplishments
- Insanity is doing the same thing over and over, expecting different results
- It's cheaper to keep her
- It's not over till it's over
- It ain't over till the fat lady sings
  (*Some versions of this modern American proverb do refer to opera, so many performances of which seem to end with a set-piece aria by a well-built soprano, but its recorded appearances are mainly connected with sport, so much so that some people are sure that is its true origin.Commentators do often say the phrase to remind people that it's the final result that matters, often in a spirit of reassurance to the supporters of the losing team.*)
- It is not so much the gift that is given but the way in which the gift is driven
- It is, what it is! (business term for the reality of the cost is what it is)
- It never rains, but it pours
- It pays to pay attention
- It takes all sorts to make a world
  (*Also, it takes all kinds to make the world go round.*)
- It takes two to make a quarrel
  (*Both parties in a quarrel should share the blame or take responsibility for it; no one can start a quarrel all by himself.*)
- It takes two to tango
- It takes two to lie, one to lie and one to listen
- It's a cracked pitcher that goes longest to the well
  (*A flawed article will require a lot of work*)

- It's a good horse that never stumbles

- It's a long lane that has no turning

- It's an ill wind that blows nobody any good
  (*A bad or evil occurrence.*)

- It's a poor job that can't stand at least one supervisor

- It's a blessing in disguise

- It's better to give than to receive

- It's better to have loved and lost than never to have loved at all

- It's Brass Monkey out there!
  (*It's very cold outside. Originates from there being three brass monkeys (see no evil, hear no evil, speak no evil). The full sentence would be "It's as cold as a brass monkey's balls.*

- It's easier to ask forgiveness than permission

- It's easy to be wise after the event

- It's never too late to mend
  (*It is never too late to correct one's mistakes or faults.*)

- It's not the size of the boat, but its vulnerability

- It's no use crying over spilt milk
  (*It is pointless to feel remorseful over a thing lost that can never be found or a mistake done that can never be corrected or rectified.*)

- It's often a person's mouth broke their nose

- It's the early bird that gets the worm

- It's the empty can that makes the most noise

- It's the squeaky wheel that gets the grease

- I wants don't gets
  (*An alternative used in the black British community is: "Ask it, Ask it don't get... Get it, get it don't want".*)

- Jack is as good as his master. His master's name is Kevin

- Jack of all trades and master of none
  (*Is a person who can do almost anything, but he rarely excels in any of them.*)

- Jam tomorrow and jam yesterday, but never jam today

- Jove but laughs at lover's perjury
- Judge not, lest ye be judged
- Just go with it
- Jack of all, master of none

- Keep a thing seven years and you will always find a use for it
- Keep no more cats than catch mice
- Keep your friends close, and your enemies closer
- Keeping up with the Joneses
- Kill not the goose that laid the golden egg
- Kill two birds with one stone
  (Accomplishing two things with a single action.)
- Knowledge is power

- Laughter is the best medicine
- Laughter is the shortest distance between two people
- Law is the solemn expression of legislative will   *Napoleon*
- Lead to Success, Follow to Failure   *Robert D*
- Learn to walk before you run
  (Do not rush into what you do not know.)
- Leave it alone and it will grow on its own
- Let him, who is without sin, cast the first stone   *Jesus Christ*
- Let bygones by bygones
  (One should consider forgiving one's and forget all the bad deeds done by others.)
- Let not the pot call the kettle black
  (A person, who has a fault, should not point out the same fault in another; do not criticize another person as you may have the same weakness.)
- Let sleeping dogs lie
  (One should preferably avoid discussing issues that are likely to create trouble.)

- Life begins at forty

- Life is too short to drink bad wine

- Life's like a box of chocolates. You never know what you're gonna get

- Life's what happens while you're making other plans

- Let us go hand in hand, not one before another

- Like cures like
  (A person can better help another if they have something in common.)

- Like father, like son, like mother, like daughter
  (Used to describe a child's behaviour when he or she acts like the father or mother.)

- Like water off a duck's back

- Little by little and bit by bit

- Little enemies and little wounds must not be despised

- Live and let Live

- Long absent, soon forgotten

- Look after the pence and the pounds will look after themselves
  (Take care of the details. (12 pence to the shilling, 20 shillings to the pound.)

- Look before you leap
  (Avoid acting hastily, without considering the possible consequences.)

- Look on the sunny side of life

- Love is a serious mental disease   *Plato*

- Love is a state in which a man sees things most decidedly as they are not   *Friedrich Nietzsche*

- Love is an irresistible desire to be irresistibly desired   *Robert Frost*

- Love is an ocean of emotions entirely surrounded by expenses   *Thomas Robert Dewar*

- Love is a great beautifier   *Louisa May Alcott*

- Love is a cunning weaver of fantasies and fables   *Sappho*

- Love is a canvas furnished by Nature and embroidered by imagination   *Voltaire*

- Love is a chain of love as nature is a chain of life *Truman Capote*

➤ Love is a friendship caught on fire   *Northern Exposure*

➤ Love is a conflict between reflexes and reflections
Mangnu Hirschfield

➤ Love is a friendship set to music   *E. Joseph Cossman*

➤ Love is a fruit in season at all times, and within reach of every hand   *Mother Teresa*

➤ Love is all you need   *Paul McCartney*

➤ Love is a better teacher than duty   *Albert Einstein*

➤ Love is a tyrant sparing none.   *Pierre Corneille*

➤ Love is all we have, the only way that each can help the other.   *Euripides*

➤ Make hay while the sun shines
(Do the task while it is possible.)

➤ Making a rod for your own back
(A rod or board would be strapped to the back to encourage the miscreant suffer for his own doings.)

➤ Man wasn't Born to suffer but to carry on

➤ Many a true word is spoken in jest

➤ Many hands make light work

➤ Many things are lost for want of asking

➤ Meaner than a junk-yard dog

➤ Measure twice, cut once

➤ Mirrors do everything we do, but they cannot think for themselves

➤ Misery loves company

➤ Money makes the mare go

➤ Money makes the world go around

➤ Money doesn't grow on trees

➤ Money talks

➤ Monkey see, Monkey do

➤ More haste less speed

- A son is a son 'til he takes him a wife; a daughter is a daughter all her life

- My father was a statesman, I'm a political woman. My father was a saint. I'm not
  Indira Gandhi

- My grandfather once told me that there were two kinds of people–those who do the work and those who take the credit. He told me to try to be in the first group; there was much less competition.
  Indira Gandhi

- My father taught me to work; he did not teach me to love it. I never did like to work, and I don't deny it. I'd rather read, tell stories, crack jokes, talk, laugh - anything but work.
  Abraham Lincoln

- Most of the things we do, we do for no better reason than that our fathers have done them or our neighbours do them, and the same is true of a larger part than what we suspect of what we think.
  Oliver Wendell Holmes, Jr

- Nature abhors a vacuum

- Nature, time and patience are three great physicians

- Necessity is the mother of invention
  (When a person is in great need of something, he will find a way of getting it.)

- No news is good news
  (When there is no news, it is likely that everything is all right.)

- Don't remove winter vests (under garments) until summer arrives

- Never judge the book by its cover

- Never put off till (until) tomorrow what you can do today

- Never let the right hand know what the left hand is doing

- Never say die
  (Never give up)

- Never say never

- Never do things by halves
  (One should not do an incomplete or imperfect job - certain tasks must not be left half done; they must be done away with immediately.)

- Never trouble trouble 'til trouble troubles you.
- New brooms sweep clean.
- Noblesse oblige
  (To be a member of the nobility carries obligations to care for the lower classes.)
- No man can serve two masters
- No man is content with his lot
- No man is an island
  (Everybody needs other people. Also everyone's actions impact others.)
- No money, no justice
- No pain, no gain
- No time like the present
- Not enough room to swing a cat
- Nothing ventured, nothing gained
- Nothing succeeds like success
- Nothing to be feared in life, but understood

- Once bitten twice shy
  (If a person has been tricked once, he will more be careful and alert the next time.)
- One man's meat is another man's poison
  (No two persons are alike-every one has his own preferences, likes and dislikes.)
- One man's terrorist is another man's freedom fighter
  Ronald Reagan.
- One murder makes a villian, millions a hero.
- Our greatest glory is not in never falling but in rising everytime we fall
  Confucius
- Out of sight... Out of mind.
- One man's meat, is another man's poison
  (What is beloved to a person is hated by someone else.)
- Opposites attract.

P

- Paddle your own canoe you lazy get
- Pain is only weakness leaving the body   ***U.S. Marines proverb***
- Patience is a virtue, possess it if you can, often found in women, never in a man!
- Penny wise, pound foolish
- Pen is mightier than the sword
- People, who live in glass houses, shouldn't throw stones
- Politics makes strange bedfellows
- Power corrupts; absolute power corrupts absolutely-Attributed to Lord Acton
- Practice makes perfect
  (It is believed that if one practices a certain skill often, he will excel in it.)
- Prior preparation prevents poor performance
- Put it in song, put it in drink; but never, ever put it in ink!
  (Reportedly said by Earl K. Long, Governor of Louisiana)
- Put a beggar on horseback and he'll ride to the devil
- Prevention is better than cure
  (It is better to be careful beforehand than to try to solve a problem after it has arisen.)
- Procrastination is the thief of time.

R

- Red sky at night: sailor's delight. Red sky in the morning: sailor take warning
  (Alternative: Red sky at night: shepherd's delight. Red sky in the morning: shepherd's warning.)
- Red to black, venom lack. Red to yellow kills a fellow
  (Meaning - A fellow describing the distinction between coral and king snakes.)
- Revenge is a dish best served cold
- Repeating a lie doesn't make it true
- A rolling stone gathers no mass

- Robbing Peter to pay Paul
  (This is quoted when one takes another loan to pay off an earlier loan) taking from one to give another.)
- Rome was not built in a day
  (Any great plan or big dream cannot be achieved overnight or easily.)
- Rules are made to be broken

- Same meat, different gravy
- Safety lies in the middle course
- Seek and ye shall find   *Christian*
- Self trust is the first secret of success
- Set a thief to catch a thief
- Simple minds think alike   *William Truong*
- Simple things please/amuse simple minds
- Six one, and half a dozen the other
  (Describes two actions with the same result, or two things that are essentially the same.)
- Silence is golden
- Smile, and the world smiles with you; cry, and you cry alone
- Something worth doing is worth doing well
  (If you are going to do something, do it right.)
- Speak of the devil and he's sure to appear
- Spare the rod and spoil the child
  (A child, who is not punished and showed the error of his ways, will become unruly.)
- Speech is silver, silence is golden
  (Talk may be beneficial, but sometimes acquiescence may be the best option to take.)
- Starve a cold; feed a fever
- Stolen fruit is the sweetest Forbidden things are the most tempting   *The Bible*
- Sticks and stones may break my bones but words will never hurt me

- Still waters run deep
  (One, who is usually silent and goes about his business quietly, may be a very wise person.)
- Strike while the iron is hot

  (Seize a good opportunity as quickly as possible.)
- Success is a journey, not a destination
- Sufficient unto the day is the evil thereof

- Talk is cheap
- Talk of the devil and he's sure to appear
- Talk the hind legs off a donkey
  (Someone who never shuts up-Often used in reference to London cab drivers.)
- Talking a mile a minute
- Talking nineteen to the dozen
- Take an old dirty, hungry, mangy, sick and wet dog and feed him and wash him and nurse him back to health, and he will never turn on you and bite you. This is how man and dog differ
- That which does not kill you, makes you stronger
- The acorn never falls far from the tree
- The ball is in your court
  (It's up to you to decide.)
- The best things come in small packages
- The best things in life are free
- The calm comes before the storm
- The coat makes the man
- The cure is worse than the disease
- The customer is always right
- The early bird gets the worm
- The end justifies the means
- The English are a nation of shopkeepers   *Napoleon*
- The longest mile is the last mile home

- The more you know, the more you know you don't know
- The only free cheese is in the mouse trap *Russian saying*
- The pen is mightier than the sword
- The way to a man's heart is through his stomach
- The weak can never forgive. Forgiveness is the attribute of the strong *Mahatma Gandhi*
- The whole is greater than its parts
- The exception proves the rule
- The first step to health is to know that we are sick
- The grass is always greener on the other side
- The head and feet keep warm, the rest will take no harm
- The key to all actions lies in belief
- The more things change, the more they stay the same
- The nail that sticks out gets pounded
- The only stupid question is the one that is not asked
- The only thing you get from picking bottoms (*i.e.,* of the stock market) is a smelly finger
- The pitcher goes too often to the well gets broken
- The proof of the pudding is in the eating
- The proof of the eating is in the size of the pudding
- The road to hell is paved with good intentions
- The squeaky wheel gets the grease
- The start of a journey should never be mistaken for success
- The teacher has not taught, until the student has learned
- The truth is in the wine.
- Possible interpretation
  (*A person will more freely divulge a secret when plied with alcohol.*)
- A drunken man's words are a sober man's thoughts
- The best is yet to come
- The value is determined by the agreement of two people
- The wish is father to the thought

- The worst good day is always better than the best bad day

- There's no such thing as a free lunch

- There are no endings only, new beginnings

- There are no small parts, only small actors

- There are three types of lies - lies, damned lies, and statistics

- There's always a calm before a storm
  Shanth

- There is only eight years betweeen success and failure in politics
  Jim Brown, Louisiana statesman

- There's a method in his madness

- There's many a slip between cup and lip
  (This comes from a Greek legend, as follows: One of the Argonauts returned from his voyage, and went home to his winery. He called for the local soothsayer, who had predicted before his voyage that he would die before he tasted another drop of his wine, from his vinery. As he finished saying this, he raised a cup filled with wine to his lips, in toast to the soothsayer, who said something in reply. Just then, he was called away to hunt a wild boar that was approaching, and died in his attempt to kill it. The phrase that the soothsayer said is translated best as – There's many a slip between the cup and the lip.)

- There's money in muck

- There's more than one way to skin a cat

- There's no accounting for taste
  Latin

- There's no arguing with the barrel of a gun

- There's no smoke without fire
  (Rumours do not spread unless there is some element of truth in them.)

- There's no peace for the wicked

- There's no place like home

- There's no time like the present

- Think before you speak

- Those, who live in glass houses, shouldn't throw stones

- Time flies – Latin
  Tempus fugit!

- Time and tide wait for none
  (Time is precious. Once it is past, no one can go back and claim it, thus everyone should be mindful of how his time is spent.)

- This, too, shall pass

- To each, his own
- To err is human, to forgive divine
  (It is only normal for man to make mistakes and do wrong, but for one to forgive another for his wrong is indeed great and gracious act.)
- To kill two birds with one stone
- Tomorrow is another day
- Too many Chiefs and not enough Indians
- Too many cooks spoil the broth
- Trapped between a rock and a hard place
- Trouble shared is trouble halved
- Truth is stranger than fiction
- Truth will out
- Try not to become a man of success but a man of value
- Two's company; three's a crowd
- Two heads are better than one
  (It is always better to get the view of another than to rely entirely on one's own judgment.)
- Two things prolong your life – A quiet heart and a loving wife
- Two wrongs don't make a right

- Up a creek without a paddle: In a situation without remedy.

- Variety is the spice of life
- Vengeance is mine, thus sayeth the Lord

- Waste not, want not
- When the going gets tough, the tough get going
- We must take the bad with the good
- Well begun is half done

- "Well done" is better than "well said"
- What a tangled web we weave, when first we practice to deceive
- What doesn't kill you makes you stronger
- What goes around comes around
  (*You will eventually have to face the consequences of your actions towards others as people tend to behave towards you as you have behaved towards others.*)
- What goes up must come down
- What you see is what you get
- What you sow is what you reap
- What's sauce for the goose is sauce for the gander
- When ignorance is bliss, 'tis folly to be wise
- Why buy the cow when you can get the milk for free?
- Willful waste makes woeful want
- Winning isn't everything
- We ourselves feel that we are doing is just a drop in the ocean, but the ocean would be less without that drop
- What's done can't be undone
  (*In life there are some things once done or decisions once made cannot be changed; malicious words once uttered or harmful actions once done cannot be taken back.*)
- When in Rome do as the Romans do
  (*When one is in a new place, country or situation, he must adapt himself to the new manners and customs.*)
- When the cat is away, the mice will play
  (*When law enforcers are not present, certain public members will take the opportunity to break the law.*)
- Where there's a will, there's a way
  (*When a person really wants to do something, he will find a way of doing it.*)

- You are responsible for you
- You can catch more flies with honey than with vinegar: Kind words/actions are more effective than harsh ones.
- You can lead a horse to water but you can't make him drink
- You can choose your friends, but you can't pick/choose your family
- You can't eat your cake and have it too
- You can't have it both ways
- You can't make an omelette without breaking eggs
- You can't make a silk purse out of a sow's ear
- You can't polish a turd
- You can't run with the hare and hunt with the hounds
- You can't take it with you when you die
- You can't teach an old dog new tricks
- You can't judge a book by its cover
- You can't win them all
- You have to crawl before you can walk
- You'll always miss 100% of the shots you don't take
- You must never confuse your feelings with your duties
- You need to bait the hook to catch the fish
- You never know what you have till it's gone
- You reap what you sow
- You scratch my back and I'll scratch yours
- You win some, you lose some

Important Proverbs From Different Countries

A

- A benevolent man should allow a few faults in himself to keep his friends in countenance *American Proverb*

- Abundance, like want, ruins many *Romanian Proverb*

- Adversity makes a man wise, not rich *Romanian Proverb*

- Advice is least heeded when most needed *English Proverb*

- After dark all cats are leopards *Native American Proverb*

- A mill cannot grind with water that is past *American Proverb*

- After lunch, rest; after dinner, walk a mile *Arab Proverb*

- After the game, the king and the pawn go into the same box *Italian Proverb*

- The afternoon knows what the morning never suspected *Swedish Proverb*

- After three days without reading, talk becomes flavurless *Chinese proverb*

- After victory, tighten your helmet chord *Japanese Proverb*

- All roads lead to Rome *Roman Proverb*

- All roads do not lead to Rome *Slovenian Proverb*

- All sins cast long shadows *Irish Proverb*

- All things good to know are difficult to learn *Greek Proverb*

- All sunshine makes the desert *Arab Proverb*

- An army of sheep led by a lion would defeat an army of lions led by a sheep *Arab Proverb*

- An ass is but an ass, though laden with gold *Romanian Proverb*

- An iron rod bends while it is hot *Greek Proverb*

- The anvil fears no blows *Romanian Proverb*

- Ask a lot, but take what is offered *Russian Proverb*

- Ask about your neighbours, then buy the house *Jewish Proverb*
- Ask the experienced rather than the learned *Arabic Proverb*
- Avoid the evil, and it will avoid thee *Gaelic Proverb*

B

- Bad is never good until worse happens *Danish Proverb*
- Be in general virtuous, and you will be happy *American Proverb*
- Beggars can never be bankrupt *American Proverb*
- Bed is the poor man's opera *Italian Proverb*
- The beginning is the half of every action *Greek Proverb*
- Be happy while you're living, For you're a long time dead *Scottish Proverb*
- Behind an able man there are always other able men *Chinese Proverb*
- Below the navel there is neither religion nor truth *Italian Proverb*
- Be not afraid of growing slowly, be afraid only of standing still *Chinese Proverb*
- Be on your guard against a silent dog and still water *Latin Proverb*
- Be prepared *Boy Scout Motto*
- Be slow in choosing a friend, but slower in changing him *Scottish Proverb*
- The best armour is to keep out of range *Italian Proverb*
- Be thine enemy an ant, see in him an elephant *Turkish Proverb*
- Better a mouse in the pot than no meat at all *Romanian Proverb*
- Better be ill spoken of by one before all than by all before one *Scottish Proverb*
- Better to light a candle than to curse the darkness *Chinese Proverb*
- Better be quarreling than lonesome *Irish Proverb*
- Between saying and doing, many a pair of shoes is worn out *Italian Proverb*
- Beware of a man of one book *English Proverb*
- Beware of a man's shadow and a bee's sting *Burmese Proverb*
- Beware of the young doctor and the old barber *Benjamin Franklin*

- The big thieves hang the little ones — *Czech Proverb*
- The blind man is laughing at the bald head — *Persian Proverb*
- A book is like a garden carried in the pocket — *Chinese Proverb*
- By asking for the impossible, obtain the best possible — *Italian Proverb*
- By learning you will teach; by teaching you will learn — *Latin Proverb*

C

- Call on God, but row away from the rocks — *Indian Proverb*
- Children are a poor man's wealth — *Danish Proverb*
- Calm weather in June, sets the corn in tune — *American Proverb*
- The church is near, but the way is icy The tavern is far, but I will walk carefully — *Ukranian Proverb*
- A closed mind is like a closed book; just a block of wood — *Chinese Proverb*
- Complain to one who can help you — *Yugoslav Proverb*
- Confessed faults are half mended — *Scottish Proverb*
- The country rooster dows not crow in the town — *African (Swahili) Proverb*
- The crow that mimics a cormorant is drowned — *Japanese Proverb*
- Cuando amor no es locura, no es amor. (When love is not madness, it is not love.) — *Spanish Proverb*

D

- Danger and delight grow on one stalk — *English Proverb*
- Deceive the rich and powerful if you will, but don't insult the — *Japanese Proverb*
- The deeper the sorrow the less tongue it hath *The Talmud*
- Deliberate often, decide once — *Latin Proverb*
- A dimple in the chin, a devil within — *Irish Proverb*
- The doctor is to be feared more than the disease — *Latin Proverb*
- The dog's kennel is not the place to keep a sausage — *Danish Proverb*
- The dog wags his tail, not for you, but for your bread — *Portuguese Proverb*

- Do not answer a fool according to his folly, or you will be like him yourself
  Miscellaneous Proverb

- Do not bathe if there is no water
  Shan Proverb

- Do not be in a hurry to tie what you cannot untie
  English Proverb

- Do not employ handsome servants
  Chinese Proverb

- Do not lengthen the quarrel while there is an opportunity of escaping
  Latin Proverb

- Do not protect yourself by a fence, but rather by your friends
  Czech Proverb

- Do not push the river, it will flow by itself
  Polish Proverb

- Do not put your spoon into the pot which does not boil for you
  Romanian Proverb

- Do not speak of a rhinoceros if there is no tree nearby
  African (Zulu) Proverb

- Do not stand in a place of danger trusting in miracles
  Arab Proverb

- Do not throw the arrow which will return against you
  Kurdish Proverb

- Do not wrong or hate your neighbour, for it is not he that you wrong but yourself
  Native American Proverb (Pima)

- Don't be too swet lest you be eaten up; don't be too bitter lest you be spewed out
  Jewish Proverb

- Don't dig your grave with your own knife and fork
  English Proverb

- Don't empty the water jar until the rain falls
  Philippine Proverb

- Don't fall before you're pushed
  English Proverb

- Don't let your sorrow come higher than your knees
  Swedish Proverb

- Don't live in a town where there are no doctors
  Jewish Proverb

- Don't make use of another's mouth unless it has been leant to you
  Belgian Proverb

- Don't offer me advice, give me money
  Spanish Proverb

- Don't open a shop unless you know how to smile
  Jewish Proverb

- Don't run too far, you will have to return the same distance
  Biblical Proverb

- Don't shake the tree when the pears fall off themselves
  Slovakian Proverb

- Don't speak unless you can improve on the silence
  Spanish Proverb
- Don't stay long when the husband is not at home
  Japanese Proverb
- Don't think there are no crocodiles because the water is calm
  Malayan Proverb
- Don't throw away the old bucket until you know whether the new one holds water
  Swedish Proverb
- Drink nothing without seeing it; Sign nothing without reading it
  Spanish Proverb
- Dwell not upon thy weariness, thy strength shall be according to the measure of thy desire
  Arab Proverb

- Each day provides its own gifts
  American Proverb
- Eat and drink with your relatives; do business with strangers
  Greek Proverb
- Eating and scratching want but a beginning
  Romanian Proverb
- Eating while seated makes one of large size; eating while standing makes one strong
  Hindu Proverb
- Employ thy time well if thou meanest to get leisure
  Benjamin Franklin
- The enemy of my enemy is my friend
  Arab Proverb
- Enjoy yourself. It's later than you think
  Chinese Proverb
- Even a clock, that does not work, is right twice a day
  Polish Proverb
- Even a fool is thought wise if he keeps silent, and discerning if he holds his tongue
  Miscellaneous Proverb
- Every animal knows more than you do
  Native American Proverb (Nez Perce)
- Every beetle is a gazelle in the eyes of its mother
  Moorish Proverb
- Every invalid is a doctor
  Irish Proverb
- Everyone thinks his own burden heavy
  French Proverb
- Every path has its puddle
  English Proverb
- Every peasant is proud of the pond in his village because from it he measures the sea
  Russian Proverb
- Every road has two directions
  Russian Proverb

- Everything passes, everything wears out, everything breaks
  (*tout passe, tout lasse, tout casse*) *French Proverb*

- Examine what is said, not him who speaks *Arab Proverb*

- Experience is the comb that nature gives us when we are bald
  Belgian proverb

- The eyes are the window of the soul *English Proverb*

- The eyes believe themselves; the ears believe other people
  German Proverb

═══╢ F ╟═══

- Fall seven times, stand up eight *Japanese Proverb*

- Feel for others, in your pocket *American Proverb*

- Folks like the truth that hits their neighbour *American Proverb*

- Fast Ripe, Fast Rotten *Japanese Proverb*

- A father is a banker provided by nature *French Proverb*

- Fear less, hope more,

  eat less, chew more,

  whine less, breathe more,

  talk less, say more,

  hate less, love more,

  and all good things will be yours *Swedish proverb*

- Fear not a jest. If one throws salt at you, you will not be harmed
  unless you have sore places *Latin Proverb*

- First deserve, and then desire *English Proverb*

- The first drink with water, the second without water, the third
  like water *Spanish Proverb*

- First secure an independent income, then practice virtue
  Greek Proverb

- Fish or cut bait *American Proverb*

- Fish, to taste good, must swim three times: in water, in butter,
  and in wine *Polish Proverb*

- A fool finds pleasure in evil conduct, but a man of understanding
  delights in wisdom *Miscellaneous Proverb*

- A fool finds no pleasure in understanding but delights in airing his own opinions   *Miscellaneous Proverb*

- A fool gives full vent to his anger, but a wise man keeps himself under control   *Miscellaneous Proverb*

- A fool shows his annoyance at once, but a prudent man overlooks an insult   *Miscellaneous Proverb*

- Forget injuries, never forget kindnesses   *Chinese Proverb*

- From a fallen tree, all make kindling   *Spanish Proverb*

- From a thorn comes a rose, and from a rose comes a thorn
                                                               Greek Proverb

- A full cup must be carried steadily   *English Proverb*

G

- Get what you can and keep what you have; that's the way to get rich   *Scottish Proverb*

- Good weight and measure, are heaven's treasure
                                                            American Proverb

- Great trees keep little ones down   *American Proverb*

- Give to a pig when it grunts and a child when it cries, and you will have a fine pig and a bad child   *Danish Proverb*

- Go and wake up your cook   *Arab Proverb*

- The go-between wears out a thousand sandals   *Japanese Proverb*

- God could not be everywhere and therefore he made mothers
                                                              Jewish Proverb

- God gives the nuts but he does not crack them   *German Proverb*

- God sells knowledge for labour. Honour for risk   *Arabic Proverb*

- God will be present, whether asked or not   *Latin Proverb*

- God gave teeth; He will give bread   *Lithuanian Proverb*

- Good fences make good neighbours   *American Proverb*

- Good men must die, but death cannot kill their names
                                                            Spanish Proverb

- Goodness shouts. Evil whispers   *Balinese Proverb*

- Goodness speaks in a whisper, evil shouts   *Tibetan proverb*

- Go often to the house of a friend; for weeds soon choke up the unused path
  Ralph Waldo Emerson

- A good painter need not give a name to his picture, a bad one must
  Polish Proverb

- Gossip needs no carriage
  Russian Proverb

- Gratitude is the heart's memory
  French Proverb

- The greater love is a mother's; then comes a dog's; then a sweetheart's
  Polish Proverb

- Great men are not always wise
  Biblical Proverb

- A guest sees more in an hour than the host in a year
  Polish Proverb

- A half-truth is a whole lie
  Jewish Proverb

- The hammer shatters glass but forges steel
  Russian Proverb

- A handful of patience is worth a bushel of brains
  Dutch Proverb

- Happiness is like a sunbeam, which the least shadow intercepts, while adversity is often as the rain of spring
  Chinese Proverb

- A heart in love with beauty never grows old
  Turkish Proverb

- The heart that loves is always young
  Greek Proverb

- He fishes well who uses a golden hook
  Latin Proverb

- He is rich who owes nothing
  French Proverb

- He, that does not ask, will never get a bargain
  French Proverb

- He, that is of a merry heart, hasth a continual feast
  Biblical Proverb

- He, that maketh haste to be rich shall not be innocent
  Biblical Proverb

- He, who is outside his door, already has a hard part of his journey behind him
  Dutch Proverb

- He, who must die, must die in the dark, even though he sells candles
  Columbian Proverb

- He, who says what he likes, will hear what he does not like
  English Proverb

- He, who searches for pearls, should not sleep
  Latin Proverb

- He, who wants a rose, must respect the thorn   *Persian Proverb*
- He, who would rule, must hear and be deaf, see and be blind
  German Proverb
- He, who asks, is a fool for five minutes, but he, who does not ask, remains a fool forever   *Chinese Proverb*
- He, who builds by the roadside, has many surveyors
  Italian Proverb
- He, who doesn't risk, never gets to drink champagne
  Russian Proverb
- He, who has health, has hope; and he who has hope, has everything   *Arab Proverb*
- He, who hurries, can not walk with dignity   *Chinese Proverb*
- He, who is not impatient, is not in love   *Italian Proverb*
- He, who knows little, quickly tells it   *Italian Proverb*
- He, who knows nothing, doubts nothing   *Italian Proverb*
- He, who puts up with insult, invites injury   *Jewish Proverb*
- He, who respects his parents, never dies   *Greek Proverb*
- He, who sows peas on the highway, does not get all the pods into his barn   *Danish Proverb*
- He, who undertakes too much, seldom succeeds   *Dutch Proverb*
- He, who would leap far, must first take a long run
  Danish Proverb
- Hide not your talents, they for use were made What's a sun dial in the shade?   *Benjamin Franklin*
- Hours are Time's shafts, and one comes winged with death
  Scottish Clock Motto

- If a man is destined to drown, he will drown even in a spoonful of water   *Yiddish Proverb*
- If Jack's in love, he's no judge of Jill's beauty   *Benjamin Franklin*
- If there is no wind, row   *Latin Proverb*
- If three people say you are an ass, put on a bridle
  Spanish Proverb
- If work were good for you, the rich would leave none for the poor
  Haitian proverb

- If you are a host to your guest, be a host to his dog also
  Russian Proverb
- If you are patient in a moment of anger, you will escape a hundred days of sorrow
  Chinese Proverb
- If you bow at all, bow low
  Chinese Proverb
- If you chase two rabbits, you will not catch either one
  Russian Proverb
- If you can't go over, you must go under
  Jewish Proverb
- If you can't lick 'em, join 'em
  American Proverb
- If you must play, decide on three things at the start: the rules of the game, the stakes, and the quitting time
  Chinese Proverb
- If you reveal your secrets to the wind, you should not blame the wind for revealing them to the trees
  Khalil Gibran
- If you see no reason for giving thanks, the fault lies in yourself
  Native American Proverb (Minquass)
- If you scatter thorns, don't go barefoot
  Italian Proverb
- If you see in your wine the reflection of a person not in your range of vision, don't drink it
  Chinese Proverb
- If you want to be respected, you must respect yourself
  Spanish Proverb
- If you want your dreams to come true, don't sleep
  Yiddish Proverb
- If you want your eggs hatched, sit on them yourself
  Haitian proverb
- If you wish good advice, consult an old man
  Romanian Proverb
- If you would be wealthy, think of saving as well as getting
  Benjamin Franklin
- If you would live healthy, be old early
  Spanish Proverb
- If you would be pope, you must think of nothing else
  Spanish Proverb
- If you suspect a man, don't employ him; and if you employ him, don't suspect him
  Chinese Proverb
- If your head is wax, don't walk in the sun
  Benjamin Franklin
- If youth but had the knowledge and old age the strength
  French Proverb
- Ignorance is bliss
  American Proverb

- In case of doubt it is best to lean to the side of mercy
  Legal Proverb
- In reviling, it is not necessary to prepare a preliminary draft
  Chinese Proverb
- In times of prosperity, friends will be plenty; in times of adversity, not one in twenty
  English Proverb
- In the kingdom of the blind, the one-eyed are kings
  Macedonian Proverb
- In the morning be first up, and in the evening last to go to bed, for they that sleep catch no fish
  English Proverb
- It is easier to pull down than to build up
  Latin Proverb
- It is not a fish until it is on the bank
  Irish Proverb
- It is not enough to aim, you must hit
  Italian Proverb
- It is the great north wind that made the Vikings
  Scandinavian Proverb
- It is the part of a good shepherd to shear his flock, not to skin it
  Latin Proverb

J

- A journey of a thousand miles begins with a single step
  Chinese Proverb
- Judge not the horse by his saddle
  Chinese Proverb

K

- Keep your broken arm inside your sleeve *Chinese Proverb*

L

- L'amour fait passer les temps. Les temps faite passer l'amour (Love makes time pass. Time makes love pass)
  French Sundial Motto
- A lean agreement is better than a fat lawsuit
  German Proverb
- Learning is a treasure that will follow its owner everywhere
  Chinese Proverb
- Let every fox take care of his own tail
  Italian Proverb
- Let him make use of instinct who cannot make use of reason
  English Proverb
- Let no man deceive you with vain words
  Biblical Proverb

- Life is not separate from death. It only looks that way
  Native American Proverb (Blackfoot)

- Listen or your tongue will keep you deaf
  Native American Proverb

- Listen to all, plucking a feather from every passing goose, but, follow no one absolutely
  Chinese Proverb

- A little pot boils easily
  Dutch Proverb

- Live together like brothers and do business like strangers
  Arab Proverb

- Live with wolves, and you learn to howl
  Spanish Proverb

- Live your own life, for you will die your own death
  Latin Proverb

- Lomhlaba Unzima, Lohmhlaba
  [This world is a harsh place, this world.]
  Zulu Proverb

- Long absent, soon forgotten
  Romanian Proverb

- Look for the good, not the evil, in the conduct of members of the family
  Jewish Proverb

- Love and eggs are best when they are fresh
  Russian Proverb

- Love is like dew that falls on both nettles and lilies
  Swedish Proverb

- Love rules without rules
  Italian Proverb

- Love tells us many things that are not so
  Ukranian Proverb

- Love your neighbour, but don't tear down your fence
  German Proverb

- The loveliest of faces are to be seen by moonlight, when one sees half with the eye and half with the fancy
  Persian Proverb

- Make happy those who are near, and those who are far will come
  Chinese Proverb

- Make sure to be in with your equals if you're going to fall out with your superiors
  Jewish Proverb

- Man has responsiblity, not power
  Native American Proverb (Tuscarora)

- A man is not where he lives, but where he loves
  Latin Proverb

➤ A man's first care should be to avoid the reproaches of his own heart, his next to escape the censures of the world
English Proverb

➤ The man who does not learn is dark, like one walking in the night
Chinese Proverb

➤ Many men know how to flatter, few men know how to praise
Greek Proverb

➤ Measure a thousand times and cut once　　*Turkish Proverb*

➤ Never advise anyone to go to war or to marry　*Spanish Proverb*

➤ Never do anything standing that you can do sitting, or anything sitting that you can do lying down
Chinese Proverb

➤ Never draw your dirk when a blow will do it　*Scottish Proverb*

➤ Never fall out with your bread and butter　*English Proverb*

➤ Never give advice in a crowd　　*Arab Proverb*

➤ Never give advice unless asked　　*German Proverb*

➤ Never rely on the glory of the morning or the smiles of your mother-in-law
Japanese Proverb

➤ Never squat with your spurs on　　*Texan Proverb*

➤ Never trust the man who tells you all his troubles but keeps from you all his joys
Jewish Proverb

➤ Never write a letter while you are angry　*Chinese Proverb*

➤ Never trouble trouble till trouble troubles you　*American Proverb*

➤ No call alligator long mouth till you pass him　*Jamaican Proverb*

➤ No need to teach an eagle to fly　　*Greek Proverb*

➤ No one can see their reflection in running water. It is only in still water that we can see
Taoist Proverb

➤ No one is rich enough to do without a neighbor　*Danish Proverb*

- ➤ Observe your enemies, for they first find your faults
  Greek Proverb
- ➤ One does evil enough when one does nothing good
  German Proverb
- ➤ One drink is just right; two is too many; three are too few
  Spanish Proverb
- ➤ One meets his destiny often in the road he takes to avoid it
  French Proverb
- ➤ One should be just as careful in choosing one's pleasures as in avoiding calamities *Chinese Proverb*
- ➤ Only mad dogs and Englishmen go out in the noon day sun
  Indian Proverb

- ➤ Pray, pray very much; but beware of telling God what you want
  French Proverb

- ➤ Ready money works great cures *French Proverb*
- ➤ The reverse side also has a reverse side *Japanese Proverb*
- ➤ A rich man has no need of character *Hebrew Proverb*

- ➤ Scratch my back and I'll scratch yours *American Proverb*
- ➤ Set a thief to catch a thief *French Proverb*
- ➤ Shared joy is a double joy; shared sorrow is half a sorrow
  Swedish Proverb
- ➤ Since the house is on fire, let us warm ourselves *Italian Proverb*
- ➤ Since we cannot get what we like, let us like what we can get
  Spanish Proverb
- ➤ A single conversation with a wise man is better than ten years of study *Chinese Proverb*
- ➤ The sinning is the best part of repentance *Arabic Proverb*
- ➤ Smooth seas do not make skillful sailors *African Proverb*

- A snake deserves no pity   *Yiddish Proverb*
- Speak of the devil and he appears   *Italian Proverb*
- Spread the table and contention will cease   *English Proverb*

- Tell me and I'll forget. Show me, and I may not remember. Involve me, and I'll understand   *Native American Proverb*
- A true friend is one that will take a bullet for you in the war   *Italian Proverb*
- Kindly submitted to quotesandsayings.com by Massimo Raimondi, from a book on Mussolini
- Tell me who's your friend and I'll tell you who you are *Russian Proverb*
- There is a pinch of the madman in every great man *French Proverb*
- There is no flying without wings*French Proverb*
- There is no pillow so soft as a clear conscience *French Proverb*
- There is nothing hidden between Heaven and Earth *Venezuelan Proverb*
- There wouldn't be such a thing as counterfeit gold if there were no real gold somewhere *Sufi Proverb*
- Those who have free seats at a play hiss first*Chinese Proverb*
- Those who sleep with dogs will rise with fleas *Italian Proverb*
- Though a tree grow ever so high, the falling leaves return to the ground *Malayan Proverb*
- Three things it is best to avoid: a strange dog, a flood, and a man who thinks he is wise*Welsh Proverb*
- To attract good fortune, spend a new coin on an old friend, share an old pleasure with a new friend, and lift up the heart of a true friend by writing his name on the wings of a dragon *Chinese Proverb*
- To change and change for the better are two different things *German Proverb*

- To deceive a diplomat, speak the truth, he has no experience with it*Greek Proverb*

- To know and to act are one and the same *Samurai Proverb*

- To know the road ahead, ask those coming back
  Chinese Proverb

- A tree never hits an automobile except in self defense
  American Proverb

- Trumpet in a herd of elephants; crow in the company of cocks; bleat in a flock of goats *Malayan Proverb*

- Turn your face to the sun and the shadows fall behind you
  Maori proverb

- Under a ragged coat lies wisdom *Romanian Proverb*

- Under a tattered cloak, you will generally find a good drinker
  Spanish Proverb

- Use power to curb power *Chinese Proverb*

- Use soft words and hard arguments *English Proverb*

- Use your enemy's hand to catch a snake *Persian Proverb*

- Vision without action is a daydream. Action without vision is a nightmare *Japanese Proverb*

- Vulnerant omnia, ultima necat. (All the [hours] wound you, the last one kills) *Latin Proverb*

- Wait until it is night before saying that it has been a fine day
  French Proverb

- Walk till the blood appears on the cheek, but not the sweat on the brow *Spanish Proverb*

- We know the worth of a thing when we have lost it
  French Proverb

- What may be done at any time will be done at no time
  Scottish Proverb

- We never know the worth of water till the well is dry
  French Proverb

➤ What the heart thinks, the tongue speaks   *Romanian Proverb*

➤ What the people believe is true
                              Native American Proverb (Anishinabe)

➤ What was hard to endure is sweet to recall   *French Proverb*

➤ What you don't see with your eyes, don't invent with your mouth
                                                        Jewish Proverb

➤ What you give you get, ten times over   *Yoruba Proverb*

➤ When a blind man carries a lame man, both go forward
                                                      Swedish Proverb

➤ When an elephant is in trouble, even a frog will kick him
                                                        Hindu Proverb

➤ When anger rises, think of the consequences   *Confucius*

➤ When a thing is done, advice comes too late   *Romanian Proverb*

➤ When eating bamboo sprouts, remember the man who planted
   them   *Chinese Proverb*

➤ When friends ask, there is no tomorrow   *Miscellaneous Proverb*

➤ When in doubt, Gallop! *Proverb of the*   *French Foreign Legion*

➤ When one shuts one eye, one does not hear everything
                                                        Swiss Proverb

➤ When spiders unite they can tie down a lion   *Ethiopian Proverb*

➤ When the fox preaches, look to the geese   *German Proverb*

➤ When there is no enemy within, the enemies outside cannot hurt
   you   *African Proverb*

➤ When two quarrel, both are to blame   *Dutch Proverb*

➤ When we cannot get what we love, we must love what is within
   our reach   *French Proverb*

➤ When you go to buy, use your eyes, not your ears   *Czech Proverb*

➤ When you have no choice, mobilize the spirit of courage
                                                        Jewish Proverb

➤ When you have only two pennies left in the world, buy a loaf of
   bread with one, and a lily with the other   *Chinese Proverb*

➤ When you throw dirt, you lose ground   *Texan Proverb*

➤ When you want to test the depth of a stream, don't use both feet
                                                      Chinese Proverb

➤ Where God has his church, the Devil will have his chapel
                                                      Spanish Proverb

- Where there is a sea, there are pirates   *Greek Proverb*
- Where there is love, there is pain   *Spanish Proverb*
- Where there are no swamps, there are no frogs   *German Proverb*
- Wheresoever you go, go with all your heart   *Confucius*
- Who depends on another man's table often dines late
        Italian Proverb
- Whoever gossips to you, will gossip about you   *Spanish Proverb*
- The whisper of a pretty girl can be heard further than the roar of a lion   *Arab Proverb*
- Who travels for love finds a thousand miles not longer than one
        Japanese Proverb
- The wise man has long ears and a short tongue   *German Proverb*
- The woman cries before the wedding and the man after
        Polish Proverb
- Words must be weighed, not counted   *Polish Proverb*

═══╫ Y ╠═══

- You may laugh at a friend's roof; don't laugh at his sleeping accommodation   *Kenyan Proverb*
- Young pigs grunt as, as old pigs grunted before them
        Danish Proverb
- Your friend has a friend; don't tell him   *Jewish Proverb*
- You can't wake a person who is pretending to be asleep
        Navajo Proverb
- You've got to do your own growing, no matter how tall your grandfather was   *Irish Proverb*

Sayings and Quotes about India

1. We owe a lot to the Indians, who taught us how to count, without which no worthwhile scientific discovery could have been made.
Albert Einstein

2. India is, the cradle of the human race, the birthplace of human speech, the mother of history, the grandmother of legend, and the great grand mother of tradition. Our most valuable and most instructive materials in the history of man are treasured up in India only.
Mark Twain

3. If there is one place on the face of earth where all the dreams of living men have found a home from the very earliest days when man began the dream of existence, it is India.
French scholar Romain Rolland

4. If there is one place on the face of this Earth where all the dreams of living men have found a home from the very earliest day when man began the dream of existence, it is India.
Romain Rolland (French Philosopher)

5. It is true that even across the Himalayan barrier, India has sent to the west such gifts as grammar and logic, philosophy and fables, hypnotism and chess, and above all numerals and the decimal system.
Will Durant (American Historian)

6. In India, I found a race of mortals living upon the Earth, but not adhering to it, inhabiting cities, but not being fixed to them, possessing everything, but possessed by nothing.
Apollonius Tyanaeus (Greek Traveller)

7. Whenever I have read any part of the Vedas, I have felt that some unearthly and unknown light illuminated me. In the great teaching of the Vedas, there is no touch of sectarianism. It is of all ages, climbs, and nationalities and is the royal road for the attainment of the Great Knowledge. When I read it, I feel that I am under the spangled heavens of a summer night.
Thoreau (American Thinker)

8.   If I were asked under what sky the human mind has most fully developed some of its choicest gifts, has most deeply pondered on the greatest problems of life, and has found solutions, I should point to India.

Max Muller (German Scholar)

9.   The Sanskrit language, whatever be its antiquity, is of wonderful structure, more perfect than the Greek, more copious than the Latin and more exquisitely refined than either.   *Sir William Jones (British Orientalist)*

10. The surgery of the ancient Indian physicians was bold and skilful. A special branch of surgery was dedicated to rhinoplasty or operations for improving deformed ears, noses and forming new ones, which European surgeons have now borrowed.   *Sir W. Hunter (British Surgeon)*

11. After the conversations about Indian philosophy, some of the ideas of Quantum Physics, that had seemed so crazy, suddenly made much more sense.

W. Heisenberg (German Physicist)

12. In the great books of India, an empire spoke to us, nothing small or unworthy, but large, serene, consistent, the voice of an old intelligence, which in another age and climate had pondered and thus disposed of the questions that exercise us.

R.W. Emerson (American Essayist)

13. In religion, India is the only millionaire......the One land that all men desire to see, and having seen once, by even a glimpse, would not give that glimpse for all the shows of all the rest of the globe combined.

Mark Twain (American Author)

14. It is already becoming clear that a chapter which had a Western beginning, will have to have an Indian ending if it is not to end in the self-destruction of the human race. At this supremely dangerous moment in history, the only way of salvation for mankind is the Indian way.

Dr. Arnold Toynbee (British Historian)

Important Facts about India

- India never invaded any country in her last 10000 years of history.

- India invented the Number System. Zero was invented by Aryabhatta.

- The World's first university was established in Takshila in 700 BC. More than 10,500 students from all over the world studied more than 60 subjects.

- The University of Nalanda, built in the 4th century CE, was one of the greatest achievements of ancient India in the field of education.

- Sanskrit is the mother of all the European languages. Sanskrit is the most suitable language for computer software - a report in Forbes magazine, July 1987.

- Ayurveda is the earliest school of medicine known to humans. Charaka, the father of medicine, consolidated Ayurveda 2500 years ago. Today Ayurveda is fast regaining its rightful place in our civilization.

- Although modern images of India often show poverty and lack of development, India was the richest country on earth until the time of British in the early 17th Century. Christopher Columbus was attracted by her wealth.

- The art of Navigation was born in the river Sindh 6000 years ago. The very word Navigation is derived from the Sanskrit word NAV GATIH. The word navy is also derived from Sanskrit 'Nou'.

- Bhaskaracharya calculated the time taken by the earth to orbit the sun hundreds of years before the astronomer Smart. Time taken by earth to orbit the sun: (5th century) 365.258756484 days.

- The value of "pi" was first calculated by Budhayana, and he explained the concept of what is known as the Pythagorean Theorem. He discovered this in the 6th century, long before the European mathematicians.

- Algebra, trigonometry and calculus came from India. Quadratic equations were propounded by Sridharacharya in the 11th century. The largest numbers the Greeks and the

Romans used were 106 whereas Hindus used numbers as big as 10**53(10 to the power of 53) with specific names as early as 5000 BCE during the Vedic period. Even today, the largest used number is Tera: 10**12(10 to the power of 12).

- According to the Gemological Institute of America, until 1896, India was the only source for diamonds to the world.

- USA based IEEE has proved what has been a century old suspicion in the world scientific community that the pioneer of wireless communication was Prof Jagdeesh Bose and not Marconi.

- The earliest reservoir and dam for irrigation was built in Saurashtra.

- According to Saka King Rudradaman I of 150 CE, a beautiful lake aptly called 'Sudarshana' was constructed on the hills of Raivataka during Chandragupta Maurya's time.

- Chess (Shataranja or AshtaPada) was invented in India.

- Sushruta is the father of surgery. 2600 years ago, he and health scientists of his time conducted complicated surgeries like cesareans, cataract, artificial limbs, fractures, urinary stones & even plastic surgery and brain surgery. Usage of anesthesia was well known in ancient India. Over 125 surgical equipments were used. Deep knowledge of anatomy, physiology, etiology, embryology, digestion, metabolism, genetics and immunity is also found in many texts.

- When many cultures were only nomadic forest dwellers over 5000 years ago, Indians established Harappan culture in Sindhu Valley (Indus Valley Civilization).

- The place value system, the decimal system was developed in India in 100 BC.

Conflicting Proverbs

There are a variety of proverbs almost everyone is familiar with. These are words of wisdom and taken by all with reverence, but some of these sayings look specious when weighed against each other.

Look at the following conflicting sayings

1. Actions speak louder than words. ⇌ The pen is mightier than the sword.
2. Knowledge is power. ⇌ Ignorance is bliss.
3. Look before you leap. ⇌ He who hesitates is lost.
4. A silent man is a wise one. ⇌ A man without words is a man without thoughts.
5. Beware of Greeks bearing gifts. ⇌ Don't look in the mouth of a gifted horse.
6. Clothes make the man. ⇌ Don't judge a book by its cover.
7. Nothing ventured, nothing gained. ⇌ Better safe than sorry.
8. Money talks. ⇌ Talk is cheap.
9. The only thing constant is change. ⇌ The more things change, the more they stay the same.
10. Two heads are better than one. ⇌ If you want something done right, do it yourself.
11. Many hands make light work. ⇌ Too many cooks spoil the broth.
12. The bigger, the better. ⇌ The best things come in small packages.
13. Absence makes the heart grow fonder. ⇌ Out of sight, out of mind.
14. What will be, will be. ⇌ Life is what you make it.
15. Cross your bridges when you come to them. ⇌ Forewarned is forearmed.
16. What's good for the goose is good for the gander. ⇌ One man's meat is another man's poison.
17. With age comes wisdom. ⇌ Out of the mouths of babes and sucklings come all wise sayings.
18. The more, the merrier. ⇌ Two's company; three's a crowd.

Proverbial Sayings and Quotes by Great Personalities

Abraham Lincoln

1. The highest art is always the most religious, and the greatest artist is always a devout person.

2. Whatever you are, be a good one.

3. Ballots are the rightful and peaceful successors to bullets.

4. There is another old poet whose name I do not now remember who said, "Truth is the daughter of Time."

5. ...Government of the people, by the people, for the people, shall not perish from the Earth.

6. Quarrel not at all. No man resolved to make the most of himself can spare time for personal contention.

7. Every man is said to have his peculiar ambition. Whether it be true or not, I can say for one that I have no other so great as that of being truly esteemed of my fellow men, by rendering myself worthy of their esteem.

8. With Malice toward none, with charity for all, with firmness in the right, as God gives us to see the right, let us strive on to finish the work we are in, to bind up the nation's wounds.

9. In the end, it's not the years in your life that count. It's the life in your years.

10. He who molds the public sentiment... makes statutes and decisions possible or impossible to make.

11. Let us have faith that right makes might, and in that faith, let us, to the end, dare to do our duty as we understand it.

12. I am not bound to win, but I am bound to be true. I am not bound to succeed, but I am bound to live by the light that I have. I must stand with anybody that stands right, and stand with him while he is right, and part with him when he goes wrong.

13. I do the very best I know how - the very best I can; and I mean to keep on doing so until the end.

14. People are just about as happy as they make up their minds to be.

15. The things I want to know are in books; my best friend is the man who'll get me a book I ain't read.

16. All I am, or can be, I owe to my angel mother.

17. Force is all-conquering, but its victories are shortlived.

18. I do not think much of a man who is not wiser today than he was yesterday.

19. America will never be destroyed from the outside. If we falter and lose our freedom, it will be because we destroyed ourselves.

20. I leave you, hoping that the lamp of liberty will burn in your bosoms until there shall no longer be a doubt that all men are created free and equal.

21. Those who deny freedom to others, deserve it not for themselves; and, under a just God, can not long retain it.

22. I am a firm believer in the people. If given the truth, they can be depended upon to meet any national crisis. The great point is to bring them the real facts.

23. You can fool some of the people all of the time, and all of the people some of the time, but you can not fool all of the people all of the time.

24. Nearly all men can stand adversity, but if you want to test a man's character, give him power.

25. It is difficult to make a man miserable while he feels worthy of himself and claims kindred to the great God who made him.

26. The probability that we may fail in the struggle ought not to deter us from the support of a cause we believe to be just.

27. I remember my mother's prayers and they have always followed me. They have clung to me all my life.

28. A woman is the only thing I am afraid of that I know will not hurt me.

29. My dream is of a place and a time where America will once again be seen as the last best hope of earth.

30. The time comes upon every public man when it is best for him to keep his lips closed.

31. Whenever I hear anyone arguing for slavery, I feel a strong impulse to see it tried on him personally.

32. The assertion that "all men are created equal" was of no practical use in effecting our separation from Great Britain and it was placed in the Declaration not for that, but for future use.

33. Character is like a tree and reputation like a shadow. The shadow is what we think of it; the tree is the real thing.

34. Always bear in mind that your own resolution to succeed is more important than any one thing.

35. To sin by silence when they should protest makes cowards of men.

36. The Lord prefers common-looking people. That is why he makes so many of them.

37. I will prepare and some day my chance will come.

38. No man has a good enough memory to be a successful liar.

39. Our defense is in the preservation of the spirit which prizes liberty as a heritage of all men, in all lands, everywhere. Destroy this spirit and you have planted the seeds of despotism around your own doors.

40. Public sentiment is everything. With public sentiment, nothing can fail. Without it, nothing can succeed.

41. He has a right to criticize, who has a heart to help.

42. I can make more generals, but horses cost money.

43. I destroy my enemies when I make them my friends.

44. It is the eternal struggle between these two principles - right and wrong. They are the two principles that have stood face to face from the beginning of time and will ever continue to struggle. It is the same spirit that says, "You work and toil and earn bread, and I'll eat it."

45. "A drop of honey catches more flies than a gallon of gal." So with men. If you would win a man to your cause, first convince him that you are his sincere friend. Therein is a drop of honey which catches his heart, which, say what he will, is the high road to his reason.

46. You are ambitious, which, within reasonable bounds, does good rather than harm.

47. Four score and seven years ago our fathers brought forth on this continent, a new nation, conceived in liberty, and dedicated to the proposition that all men are created equal.

48. The Bible is not my book and Christianity is not my religion. I could never give assent to the long complicated statements of Christian dogma.

49. Any people anywhere, being inclined and having the power, have the right to rise up, and shake off the existing government, and form a new one that suits them better. This is a most valuable - a most sacred right - a right, which we hope and believe, is to liberate the world.

50. Am I not destroying my enemies when I make friends of them?

51. The dogmas of the quiet past are inadequate to the stormy present. The occasion is piled high with difficulty, and we must rise with the occasion. As our case is new, so we must think anew and act anew.

52. I am a firm believer in the people. If given the truth, they can be depended upon to meet any national crisis. The great point is to bring them the real facts.

Alexander The Great

1. A tomb now suffices him for whom the whole world was not sufficient.

2. I would rather excel others in the knowledge of what is excellent than in the extent of my powers and dominion.

3. I am dying from the treatment of too many physicians.

4. How great are the dangers I face to win a good name in Athens.

5. Remember, upon the conduct of each depends the fate of all.

6. In faith and hope the world will disagree, but all mankind's concern is charity.

7. There is nothing impossible to him who will try.

Aristotle

1. We praise a man who feels angry on the right grounds and against the right persons and also in the right manner at the right moment and for the right length of time.

2. To the query, "What is a friend?" his reply was "A single soul dwelling in two bodies."

3. If happiness is activity in accordance with excellence, it is reasonable that it should be in accordance with the highest excellence.

4. No great genius has ever existed without some touch of madness.

5. All men by nature desire knowledge.

6. The moral virtues, then, are produced in us neither by nature nor against nature. Nature, indeed, prepares in us the ground for their reception, but their complete formation is the product of habit.

7. The generality of men are naturally apt to be swayed by fear rather than reverence, and to refrain from evil rather because of the punishment that it brings than because of its own foulness.

8. For as the interposition of a rivulet, however small, will occasion the line of the phalanx to fluctuate, so any trifling disagreement will be the cause of seditions; but they will not so soon flow from anything else as from the disagreement between virtue and vice, and next to that between poverty and riches.

9. Inferiors revolt in order that they may be equal, and equals that they may be superior. Such is the state of mind which creates revolutions.

10. What the statesman is most anxious to produce is a certain moral character in his fellow citizens, namely a disposition to virtue and the performance of virtuous actions.

11. Plato is dear to me, but dearer still is truth.

12. Wit is educated insolence.

Albert Einstein

1. "Great spirits have always encountered violent opposition from mediocre minds."

2. "Whoever undertakes to set himself up as judge in the field of truth and knowledge is shipwrecked by the laughter of the Gods."

3. "When I examine myself and my methods of thought, I come to the conclusion that the gift of fantasy has meant more to me than my talent for absorbing positive knowledge."

4. "The secret to creativity is knowing how to hide your sources."

5. "The only source of knowledge is experience."

6. "The intuitive mind is a sacred gift and the rational mind is a faithful servant. We have created a society that honours the servant and has forgotten the gift."

7. "I am enough of an artist to draw freely upon my imagination. Imagination is more important than knowledge. Knowledge is limited. Imagination encircles the world."

8. "We should take care not to make the intellect our god; it has, of course, powerful muscles, but no personality."

9. "The important thing is not to stop questioning. Curiosity has its own reason for existing. One cannot help but be in awe when he contemplates the mysteries of eternity, of life, of the marvellous structure of reality. It is enough if one tries merely to comprehend a little of this mystery every day. Never lose a holy curiosity."

10. "Reading, after a certain age, diverts the mind too much from its creative pursuits. Any man, who read too much and uses his own brain too little, falls into lazy habits of thinking."

11. "Intelligence makes clear to us the inter-relationship of means and ends. But mere thinking cannot give us a sense of the ultimate and fundamental ends. To make clear these fundamental ends and valuations and to set them fast in the emotional life of the individual, seems to me precisely the most important function which religion has to form in the social life of man."

12. "During the last century, and part of the one before, it was widely held that there was an unreconcilable conflict between knowledge and belief. The opinion prevailed amoung advanced minds that it was time that belief should be replaced increasingly by knowledge; belief that did not itself rest on knowledge was superstition, and as such had to be opposed. According to this conception, the sole function of education was to open the way to thinking and knowing, and the school, as the outstanding organ for the people's education, must serve that end exclusively." Quoting Newton.

13. "Knowledge of what is does not open the door directly to what should be. If one asks the whence derives the authority of fundamental ends, since they cannot be stated and justifed merely by reason, one can only answer: they exist in a healthy society as powerful traditions, which act upon the conduct and aspirations and judgements of the individuals; they are there, that is, as something living, without its being necessary to find justification for their existence. They come into being not through demonstration but through revelation, through the medium of powerful personalities. One must not attempt to justify them, but rather to sense their nature simply and clearly."

Charles Dickens

1. A loving heart is the truest wisdom.

2. Have a heart that never hardens, and a temper that never tires, and a touch that never hurts.

3. A day wasted on others is not wasted on one's self.

4. It was the best of times, it was the worst of times.

5. Electric communication will never be a substitute for the face of someone who with their soul encourages another person to be brave and true.

6. A wonderful fact to reflect upon, that every human creature is constituted to be that profound secret and mystery to every other.

7. If there were no bad people, there would be no good lawyers.

8. The pain of parting is nothing to the joy of meeting again.

9. I have known a vast quantity of nonsense talked about bad men not looking you in the face. Don't trust that conventional idea.

10. Dishonesty will stare honesty out of countenance any day in the week, if there is anything to be got by it.

11. Papa, potatoes, poultry, prunes and prism, are all very good words for the lips.

12. I never could have done what I have done without the habits of punctuality, order, and diligence, without the determination to concentrate myself on one subject at a time.

13. This is a world of action, and not for moping and droning in.

14. Vices are sometimes only virtues carried to excess!

15. Any man may be in good spirits and good temper when he's well dressed. There ain't much credit in that.

16. If you could see my legs when I take my boots off, you'd form some idea of what unrequited affection is.

17. The whole difference between construction and creation is exactly this: that a thing constructed can only be loved after it is constructed; but a thing created is loved before it exists.

18. Do you spell it with a "V" or a "W"?' inquired the judge. 'That depends upon the taste and fancy of the speller, my Lord'.

19. Reflect upon your present blessings, of which every man has plenty; not on your past misfortunes of which all men have some.

20. It opens the lungs, washes the countenance, exercises the eyes, and softens down the temper; so cry away.

21. Minds, like bodies, will often fall into a pimpled, ill-conditioned state from mere excess of comfort.

22. I only ask to be free. The butterflies are free.

23. Most men are individuals no longer so far as their business, its activities, or its moralities are concerned. They are not units but fractions.

24. There is a wisdom of the head, and a wisdom of the heart.

25. Life is made of ever so many partings welded together.

26. There is nothing so strong or safe in an emergency of life as the simple truth.

27. To conceal anything from those to whom I am attached, is not in my nature. I can never close my lips where I have opened my heart.

28. The one great principle of English law is to make business for itself.

29. I revere the memory of Mr. F. as an estimable man and most indulgent husband, only necessary to mention Asparagus and it appeared or to hint at any little delicate thing to drink and it came like magic in a pint bottle; it was not ecstasy but it was comfort.

30. No one is useless in this world who lightens the burden of it to anyone else.

31. The men who learn endurance, are they who call the whole world, brother.

Leo Nikolaevich Tolstoy

1. I know that my unity with all people cannot be destroyed by national boundaries and government orders.

2. Love is life. All, everything that I understand, I understand only because I love.

   And all people live, Not by reason of any care they have for themselves, but by the love for them that is in other people.

3. All violence consists in some people forcing others, under threat of suffering or death, to do what they do not want to do.

4. Everyone thinks of changing the world, but no one thinks of changing himself.

5. A man can live and be healthy without killing animals for food; therefore, if he eats meat, he participates in taking animal life merely for the sake of his appetite.

6. What a strange illusion it is to suppose that beauty is goodness.

7. The two most powerful warriors are patience and time.

8. All happy families resemble one another, each unhappy family is unhappy in its own way.

9. Historians are like deaf people who go on answering questions that no one has asked them.

10. In all history there is no war which was not hatched by the governments, the governments alone, independent of the interests of the people, to whom war is always pernicious even when successful.

Man lives consciously for himself, but is an unconscious instrument in the attainment of the historic, universal aims of humanity.

11. Art is not a handicraft, it is the transmission of feeling the artist has experienced.

12. We lost because we told ourselves we lost.

13. There is only one time that is important - NOW! It is the most important time because it is the only time that we have any power.

14. Government is an association of men who do violence to the rest of us.

15. Faith is the sense of life, that sense by virtue of which man does not destroy himself, but continues to live on. It is the force whereby we live.

16. Our body is a machine for living. It is organized for that, it is its nature. Let life go on in it unhindered and let it defend itself.

17. War is so unjust and ugly that all who wage it must try to stifle the voice of conscience within themselves.

18. True life is lived when tiny changes occur.

19. In the name of God, stop a moment, cease your work, look around you.

20. Even in the valley of the shadow of death, two and two do not make six.

21. To say that a work of art is good, but incomprehensible to the majority of men, is the same as saying of some kind of food that it is very good but that most people can't eat it.

22. War on the other hand is such a terrible thing, that no man, especially a Christian man, has the right to assume the responsibility of starting it.

23. What an immense mass of evil must result... from allowing men to assume the right of anticipating what may happen.

24. The greater the state, the more wrong and cruel its patriotism, and the greater is the sum of suffering upon which its power is founded.

25. There is no greatness where there is no simplicity, goodness and truth.

26. Truth, like gold, is to be obtained not by its growth, but by washing away from it all that is not gold.

27. The law condemns and punishes only actions within certain definite and narrow limits; it thereby justifies, in a way, all similar actions that lie outside those limits.

28. One of the first conditions of happiness is that the link between Man and Nature shall not be broken.

29. The sole meaning of life is to serve humanity.

Arthur Miller

1. Without alienation, there can be no politics.

2. My conception of the audience is of a public, each member of which is carrying about with him what he thinks is an anxiety, or a hope, or a preoccupation which is his alone and isolates him from mankind; and in this respect at least the function of a play is to reveal him to himself so that he may touch others by virtue of the revelation of his mutuality with them. If only for this reason I regard the theatre as a serious business, one that makes or should make man more human, which is to say, less alone.

3. Look, we're all the same; a man is a fourteen-room house in the bedroom he's asleep with his intelligent wife, in the living-room he's rolling around with some bareass girl, in the library he's paying his taxes, in the yard he's raising tomatoes, and in the cellar he's making a bomb to blow it all up.

4. If you complain of people being shot down in the streets, of the absence of communication or social responsibility, of the rise of everyday violence which people have become accustomed to, and the dehumanization of feelings, then the ultimate development on an organized social level is the concentration camp. . . . The concentration camp is the final expression of human separateness and its ultimate consequence. It is organized abandonment.

5. A good newspaper, I suppose, is a nation talking to itself.

6. Maybe all one can do is hope to end up with the right regrets.

7. Success, instead of giving freedom of choice, becomes a way of life. There's no country I've been to where people, when you come into a room and sit down with them, so often ask you, "What do you do?" And, being American, many's the time I've almost asked that question, then realized it's good for my soul not to know. For a while! Just to let the evening wear on and see what I think of this person without knowing what he does and how successful he is, or what a failure. We're ranking everybody every minute of the day.

8. By whatever means it is accomplished, the prime business of a play is to arouse the passions of its audience so that by the route of passion, may be opened up new relationships between a man and men, and between men and Man. Drama is akin to the other inventions of man in that it ought to help us to know more, and not merely to spend our feelings.

9. A playwright . . . is . . . the litmus paper of the arts. He's got to be, because if he isn't working on the same wave length as the audience, no one would know what in hell he was talking about. He is a kind of psychic journalist, even when he's great.

10. The closer a man approaches tragedy, the more intense is his concentration of emotion upon the fixed point of his commitment, which is to say the closer he approaches what in life we call fanaticism.

Maya Angelou

1. For Africa to me . . . is more than a glamorous fact. It is a historical truth. No man can know where he is going unless he knows exactly where he has been and exactly how he arrived at his present place.

2. The fact that the adult American Negro female emerges a formidable character is often met with amazement, distaste and even belligerance. It is seldom accepted as an inevitable outcome of the struggle won by survivors, and deserves respect if not enthusiastic acceptance.

3. I love to see a young girl go out and grab the world by the lapels. Life's a bitch. You've got to go out and kick ass.

4. The quality of strength lined with tenderness is an unbeatable combination, as are intelligence and necessity when unblunted by formal education.

5. Children's talent to endure stems from their ignorance of alternatives.

6. I find it interesting that the meanest life, the poorest existence, is attributed to God's will, but as human beings become more affluent, as their living standard and style begin to ascend the material scale, God descends the scale of responsibility at a commensurate speed.

7. We allow our ignorance to prevail upon us and make us think we can survive alone, alone in patches, alone in groups, alone in races, even alone in genders.

8. At fifteen, life had taught me undeniably that surrender, in its place, was as honorable as resistance, especially if one had no choice.

9. Self-pity in its early stage is as snug as a feather mattress. Only when it hardens does it become uncomfortable.

10. As far as I knew white women were never lonely, except in books. White men adored them, Black men desired them and Black women worked for them.

Mark Twain

1. By trying we can easily learn to endure adversity. Another man's, I mean.

2. The man who is a pessimist before 48 knows too much; if he is an optimist after it, he knows too little.

3. India has 2,000,000 gods, and worships them all. In religion, other countries are paupers; India is the only millionaire.

4. We have not all had the good fortune to be ladies. We have not all been generals, or poets, or statesmen; but when the toast works down to the babies, we stand on common ground.

5. There was never yet an uninteresting life. Such a thing is an impossibility. Inside of the dullest exterior there is a drama, a comedy, and a tragedy.

6. A classic is something that everybody wants to have read and nobody wants to read. There comes a time in every rightly constructed boy's life when he has a raging desire to go somewhere and dig for hidden treasure.

7. Put all your eggs in the one basket and WATCH THAT BASKET.

8. To arrive at a just estimate of a renowned man's character, one must judge it by the standards of his time, not ours.

9. There is nothing you can say in answer to a compliment. I have been complimented myself a great many times, and they always embarrass me. I always feel that they have not said enough.

10. It could probably be shown by facts and figures that there is no distinctly native American criminal class except Congress.

11. What, then, is the true Gospel of consistency? Change. Who is the really consistent man? The man who changes. Since change is the law of his being, he cannot be consistent if he stick in a rut.

12. War talk by men who have been in a war is always interesting; whereas moon talk by a poet who has not been in the moon is likely to be dull.

13. Man is the only animal that blushes. Or needs to.

14. Man will do many things to get himself loved, he will do all things to get himself envied. Few things are harder to put up with than the annoyance of a good example.

15. Wrinkles should merely indicate where smiles have been.

16. Let us be thankful for the fools. But for them the rest of us could not succeed.

17. It takes your enemy and your friend, working together, to hurt you to the heart – the one to slander you and the other to get the news to you.

18. The very ink in which history is written is merely fluid prejudice.

19. True irreverence is disrespect for another man's god.

20. Grief can take care of itself, but to get the full value of a joy, you must have somebody to divide it with.

21. Nothing that grieves us can be called little—by the eternal laws of proportion a child's loss of a doll and a king's loss of a crown are events of the same size.

22. Martyrdom covers a multitude of sins.

23. The man with a new idea is a crank until the idea succeeds.

24. There is no sadder sight than a young pessimist, except an old optimist.

25. My books are water; those of the great geniuses is wine. Everybody drinks water.

26. Get your facts first, and then you can distort them as much as you please.

27. The radical invents the views. When he has worn them out the conservative adopts them.

28. When angry, count four; when very angry, swear.

D.H. Lawrence

1. I believe a man is born first unto himself – for the happy developing of himself, while the world is a nursery, and the pretty things are to be snatched for, and pleasant things tasted; some people seem to exist thus right to the end. But most are born again on entering manhood; then they are born to humanity, to a consciousness of all the laughing, and the never-ceasing murmur of pain and sorrow that comes from the terrible multitudes of brothers.

2. An artist is only an ordinary man with a greater potentiality – same stuff, same make up, only more force. And the strong driving force usually finds his weak spot, and he goes cranked, or goes under.

3. It is so much more difficult to live with one's body than with one's soul. One's body is so much more exacting – what it won't have it won't have, and nothing can make bitter into sweet.

4. One sheds one's sicknesses in books – repeats and presents again one's emotions, to be master of them.

5. I can't bear art that you can walk round and admire. A book should be either a bandit or a rebel or a man in the crowd.

6.   The human consciousness is really homogeneous. There is no complete forgetting, even in death.

7.   I believe that a man is converted when first he hears the low, vast murmur of life, of human life, troubling his hitherto unconscious self.

8.   Brute force crushes many plants. Yet the plants rise again. The Pyramids will not last a moment compared with the daisy. And before Buddha or Jesus spoke the nightingale sang, and long after the words of Jesus and Buddha are gone into oblivion, the nightingale still will sing. Because it is neither preaching nor commanding nor urging. It is just singing. And in the beginning was not a Word, but a chirrup.

9.   This is the very worst wickedness, that we refuse to acknowledge the passionate evil that is in us. This makes us secret and rotten.

10. The only justice is to follow the sincere intuition of the soul – angry or gentle. Anger is just, and pity is just, but judgement is never just.

11. One could laugh at the world better if it didn't mix tender kindliness with its brutality.

12. We only seem to learn from Life that Life doesn't matter so much as it seemed to do – it's not so burningly important, after all, what happens. We crawl, like blinking sea-creatures, out of the ocean onto a spur of rock, we creep over the promontory bewildered and dazzled and hurting ourselves, then we drop in the ocean on the other side; and the little transit doesn't matter so much.

13. A man has no religion who has not slowly and painfully gathered one together, adding to it, shaping it; and one's religion is never complete and final, it seems, but must always be undergoing modification.

14. The human being is a most curious creature. He thinks he has got one soul, and he has got dozens.

15. Be still when you have nothing to say; when genuine passion moves you, say what you've got to say, and say it hot.

16. I cannot cure myself of that most woeful of youth's follies – thinking that those, who care about us, will care for the things that mean much to us.

***Bruce Lee-the famous martial artist and
film star (Deceased)***

1. Empty your mind, be formless, shapeless – like water.

    Now you put water into a cup, it becomes the cup;

    You put water into a bottle, it becomes the bottle;

    You put it in a teapot, it becomes the teapot.

    Now water can *flow* or it can *crash*!

    Be water, my friend.

2. When the opponent expand, I contract;

    When he contracts, I expand;

    And when there is an opportunity,

    I do not hit – it hits all by itself.

3. As long as we separate this "oneness" into two, we won't achieve realisation.

4. Not being tense but ready. Not thinking but not dreaming. Not being set but flexible. Liberation from the uneasy sense of confinement. It is being wholly and quietly alive, aware and alert, ready for whatever may come.

5. Knowing is not enough; we must apply. Willing is not enough; we must do.

6. A good teacher protects his pupils from his own influence.

7. True refinement seeks simplicity.

8. Ideas are the beginning of all achievement.

9. If you want to do your duty properly, you should do just a little more than that.

10. A goal is not always meant to be reached, it often serves simply as something to aim at.

11. One great cause of failure is lack of concentration.

Bhagavad Gita

1. No matter what conditions you encounter in life, your right is only to the works – not to the fruits thereof. You should not be impelled to act for selfish reasons, nor should you be attached to inaction.

2. Whenever virtue declines and unrighteousness rises, I manifest Myself as an embodied being. To protect the Saints and Sages, to destroy the evil-doers and to establish Dharma (righteousness), I am born from age to age.

3. Seeing your great form with many faces, many eyes, many arms, many thighs and feet, and many terrible tusks and stomachs, O Mighty Armed, the worlds are terrified and so am I.

4. I am pleased to see this universal form which was never seen by me before, and at the same time my mind is terrified with fear. Therefore, please reveal to me Your previous form. O God of Gods, O Refuge of the Universe, be gracious to me.

5. To those who are constantly devoted and worship Me with love, I give the understanding by which they can come to Me.

6. Out of compassion for them, I, dwelling in their hearts, destroy with the shining lamp of knowledge the darkness born of ignorance.

7. Having seen this terrible form of Mine, do not be afraid or bewildered. Rid of fear, with a cheeful heart, now behold again My previous form.

8. Arjun said: O Janardana, having beheld Your human form, I am now free of fear, my mind is composed, I have resumed by normal awareness.

9. Picking up his conch, the golden Devadatta, Arjun blew on it fiercely; the heavens echoed with the noise, and the chariot warriors stood petrified on the field. Their horses stood paralysed, with eyes wide open ...

10. O Countless formed Divinity, You are the First of the Gods, the Supreme Being, the Ancient Self, and You are the resting place of the world. You are the knower, the knowable, and the Supreme Abode of Lord Vishnu. This entire world is pervaded by You.

11. O God of Incomparable Power, You are the Father of this creation consisting of movables and immovables. You are the Adorable One, The Preceptor, and the Glorious One. There is no equal to You in the three worlds, much less can any one excel You.

12. Krishna said,"Do you duty, Arjun, as your nature dictates. All work fetters, as all fire gives smoke. Only selfless duty saves. Fix your mind on me. Surrender all deeds to me. All problems will be solved by my grace. Pride will lead only to your moral ruin. If, filled with pride, you say, 'I will not fight,' it is all in vain. You are foolish. Fight you will, your nature will make you fight. Your karma will make you fight. You will fight in spite of yourself."

13. The Blessed Lord said: You are grieving over those who are not fit to be grieved for, yet you speak words like a great man of wisdom. But the wise do not grieve neither over the living nor over the dead. Never did I not exist, nor did you nor these kings. Nor shall we ever cease to exist in the future.

14. Krishna drove the white-horsed chariot to where Bhishma stood, shining like the sun. Obscured by an arrowy shower from Bhishma, Arjun's chariot was hidden from view, but Krishna, with great skill and patience, drove the wounded horse through. With his cloud-booming Gandiva bow, Arjun shot Bhishma's bow out of his hands.

15. Urged on by Krishna, Arjun displayed his full prowess. He seemed like the Destroyer himself at the end of creation. Many heroes, hoping to win glory and with death as their goal, came befoe Arjun as he let loose his shafts. They fell by the thousands. Arjun carved a path through the Kauravas.

16. Krishna drove the horses forward and the fine chariot moved into the center of the field. Krishna smiled, "Just behold, O Arjun, all the Kurus assembled here." Arjun looked across the field. Krishna could understand Arjun's mind. The long-awaited time for war had arrived – a terrible fratricidal war. There was now no turning back. Suddenly seeing the horror of it before him, Arjun gazed at his relatives and friends arrayed across from him—men who were like fathers, brothers, sons, and grandsons, as well as teachers, uncles, friends, in-laws, and well-wishers.

17. Life without Krishna has no joy for me. Tell me what is good for me. I am a wanderer with a hollow heart.

18. Arjun chose Krishna, though Krishna had vowed to lay down his arms on the battlefield ...

... Krishna asked: "Why did you pick me, knowing I would not fight?"

"I can handle the soldiers myself, O Krishna, if I have your presence to give me moral support. Some of your glory will surely rub off on me."

19. Krishna threw down the reins and leapt from the chariot. Taking up a nearby chariot wheel, he raised it above his head as if it were his own favourite weapon, the Sudarshan chakra. He ran toward Bhishma as a lion might run at an elephant. The end of his yellow silk garment fluttered in the dusty air, resembling lightning dancing in a dark cloud. The wheel in his hand seemed to glow with his own effulgence, and it looked as beautiful as the primeval lotus from which Brahma was born. Krishna's dark arm appeared like the stalk of the lotus, and his charming face, covered with beads of perspiration, was its filament.

20. Pandu's sons sat silently, overtaken with affection for their dying grandfather. Seeing this, Bhishmadeva was himself overwhelmed with love. Tears sprang to his eyes and he said, trembling, "Oh, my dear son Yudhisthir, what terrible sufferings and injustices you good souls have suffered, even though you are the son of religion personified. Only because you were protected by the brahmins, religion and the Supreme Lord himself, did you manage to survive."

21. The Blessed Lord said: This form of Mine that you have seen is very difficult to behold; even gods are ever desirous of beholding this form.

22. O Arjun, the scorcher of your foes, it is by single minded devotion alone that I can be known, seen in reality, and also entered into. O Son of Pandu, he who performs actions for Me, who considers Me as the Supreme Goal, who is My devotee, and is devoid of attachments; who is without animosity towards all living beings, he alone attains Me.

23. Deciding to surrender himself to whatever Krishna advised, Arjun said,"O Krishna, I am confused about my duty and have lost all composure due to weakness of heart. Surely I am being consumed by miserly and selfish considerations, but I am not able to overcome them. In this condition I ask you to please tell me what is best for me. Now I am your disciple and a soul surrendered unto you. Please instruct me. I can see no means to drive away this grief. Even winning a prosperous kingdom equal to that of the gods will not assuage my sorrow. O Govinda, I will not fight."

24. Krishna now smiled more broadly. he was pleased that Arjun, his dear friend, was ready to accept him as teacher and guide. Holding up his hand in blessing, he said, "Although you are speaking learned words from the scriptures, you are still mourning for something unworthy of grief. A wise man laments neither for the living nor the dead. Both you, I and all these assembled kshatriyas have always existed and will always exist. We are eternal souls, passing from body to body.

25. He who sees me in all things, and all things in me, is never far from me, and I am never far from him.

26. "O Krishna, son of Devaki,

   Lord of the universe, of inexhaustible powers,

   Krishna of the blue-lotus skin,

   Krishna of the white-lily eyes,

   Saffron-robed Krishna,

   Help me now!"   *Draupadi's cry to Krishna*

27. "What will you do if Karna is able to kill me?" Arjun asked Krishna. Krishna smiled and replied, "The sun will fall, the earth shatter into a thousand fragments, and fire lose its heat before he kills you. But if he does, it is a sign that the end of the world has come. As for me, I shall kill him with my bare hands."

28. Wherever there is Krishna, the Lord of Yoga, and wherever there is Arjun, the wielder of the bow, there will indeed abide prosperity, victory, glory, and righteousness; this is my firm conviction.   *Bhagavad Gita*

Bill Gates

1. The great thing about a computer notebook is that no matter how much you stuff into it, it doesn't get bigger or heavier.

2. Your most unhappy customers are your greatest source of learning.

3. Often you have to rely on intuition.

4. The first rule of any technology used in a business is that automation applied to an efficient operation will magnify the efficiency. The second is that automation applied to an inefficient operation will magnify the inefficiency.

5. We always overestimate the change that will occur in the next two years and underestimate the change that will occur in the next ten. Don't let yourself be lulled into inaction.

6. 640K ought to be enough for anybody.

7. I don't think there's anything unique about human intelligence. All the neurons in the brain, that make up perceptions and emotions, operate in a binary fashion.

8. Perhaps the most truthful on Microsoft marketing :
"There won't be anything we won't say to people to try and convince them that our way is the way to go."

9. "If you can't make it good, at least make it look good."

10. "I believe OS/2 is destined to be the most important operating system, and possibly program, of all time. As the successor to DOS, which has over 10,000,000 systems in use, it creates incredible opportunities for everyone involved with PCs."

11. "There are people who don't like capitalism, and people who don't like PCs. But there's no-one who likes the PC who doesn't like Microsoft."

12. Microsoft has not changed any of its plans for Windows. It is obvious that we will not include things like threads and preemptive multitasking in Windows. By the time we added that, you would have OS/2.

13. Interviewer : Is studying computer science the best way to prepare to be a programmer?

14. Gates : No, the best way to prepare is to write programs, and to study great programs that other people have written. In my case, I went to the garbage cans at the Computer Science Center and fished out listings of their operating system.

15. Microsoft programs are generally bug-free. If you visit the Microsoft hotline, you'll literally have to wait weeks if not months until someone calls in with a bug in one of our programs. 99.99% of calls turn out to be user mistakes.

16. I know not a single less irrelevant reason for an update than bugfixes. The reasons for updates are to present more new features

17. "Bill [Gates] is just smarter than everyone else," Mike Maples, an executive vice-president of Microsoft, says, "There are probably more smart people per square foot right here than anywhere else in the world, but Bill is just smarter."

Bill Gates—advice for kids

To anyone with kids of any age, or anyone who has ever been a kid, here's some advice Bill Gates dished out at a high school speech about 11 things they did not learn in school.

Rule 1 : Life is not fair...get used to it.

Rule 2 : The world won't care about your self-esteem. The world will expect you to accomplish something BEFORE you feel good about yourself.

Rule 3 : You will NOT make 40 thousand dollars a year right out of high school. You won't be a vice-president with a car phone, until you earn both.

Rule 4 : If you think your teacher is tough, wait till you get a boss. He doesn't have tenure.

Rule 5 : Flipping burgers is not beneath your dignity. Your grandparents had a different word for burger flipping – they called it opportunity.

Rule 6 : If you mess up, it's not your parents' fault, so don't whine about your mistakes, learn from them.

Rule 7 : Before you were born, your parents weren't as boring as they are now. They got that way from paying your bills, cleaning your clothes and listening to you talk about how cool you are. So before you save the rain forest from the parasites of your parents' generation, try delousing the closet in your own room.

Rule 8 : Your school may have done away with winners and losers but life has not. In some schools they have abolished failing grades and they'll give you as many times as you want to get the right answer. This doesn't bear the slightest resemblance to ANYTHING in real life.

Rule 9 : Life is not divided into semesters. You don't get summers off and very few employers are interested in helping you find yourself. You have to do that on your own time.

Rule 10 : Television is NOT real life. In real life, people actually have to leave the coffee shop and go to jobs.

Rule 11 : Be nice to nerds. Chances are you'll end up working for one.

Oscar Wilde

1. Women are sphinxes without secrets.

2. American women are pretty and charming – little oases of elegant unreasonableness in a vast desert of practical common sense.

3. All women become like their mothers, that is their tragedy; no man does, that is his.

4. Never trust a woman who tells you her real age; a woman who tells you that, would tell you anything.

5. Women are meant to be loved, not understood.

6. A woman will flirt with anyone in the world, so long as other women are looking on.

7. Women can discover everything except the obvious.

8. Crying is the refuge of plain women and the ruin of pretty ones.

9. If you really want to know what a woman means, which is dangerous, always look at her but never listen.

10. Women give to men the very gold of their lives; but they always want it back in small change.

11. I like men who have a future, and women who have a past.

12. If a man is a gentleman, he knows quite enough, and if he is not a gentleman, whatever he knows is likely to be bad for him.

13. The world was made for men and not for women.

14. I sometimes think that God, in creating man, rather overestimated His ability.

15. A man can be happy with any woman, so long as he does not love her.

16. The happiness of a married man depends on the people he has not married.

17. The husbands of very beautiful women usually belong to the criminal classes.

18. The only real tragedy in a woman's life is that her past is always her lover, and the future is invariably her husband.

19. In married life, three is company, two is none.

20. The proper basis for a marriage is mutual misunderstanding.

21. There is nothing in the world like the devotion of a married woman, it's a thing that no married man knows anything about.

22. When a woman marries again, it is because she detested her first husband; when a man marries again; it is because he adored his first wife. Women try their luck, men risk theirs.

23. I have always been of the opinion that a man about to get married should know either everything or nothing.

24. Men marry because they are tired, women because they are curious; both are disappointed.

25. Anyone can sympathize with the sufferings of a friend; it requires a very fine nature to sympathize with a friend's success.

26. A little sincerity is a dangerous thing, and a great deal of it is absolutely fatal.

27. Education is a wonderful thing, provided you always remember that nothing worth knowing can ever be taught.

28. It is a very sad thing that nowadays there is so little useless information around.

29. Ignorance is a rare exotic fruit; touch it, and the bloom has gone.

30. The only duty we owe history is to rewrite it.

31. Democracy is simply the bludgeoning of the people, for the people, by the people.

32. Work is the curse of the drinking classes.

33. I find that alcohol, taken in sufficient quantities, produces all the effects of intoxication.

34. Consistency is the last refuge of the unimaginative.

35. A cynic is a man who knows the price of everything but the value of nothing.

36. Fashion is what one wears oneself; what is unfashionable is what other people wear.

37. No great artist ever sees things as they really are; if he did, he would cease to be an artist.

38. Society often forgives the criminal but it never forgives the dreamer.

39. Thre is no such thing as a moral or immoral book; books are well written or badly written.

40. Examinations consist of the foolish asking questions the wise cannot answer.

41. Punctuality is the thief of time.

42. The truth is rarely pure and never simple.

43. The book of life begins with a man and woman in a garden; it ends with revelations.

44. The good end happily and the bad unhappily; that is what fiction means.

45. We are all in the gutter, but some of us are looking at the stars.

46. Experience is the name we all give to our mistakes.

47. The only thing worse in the world than being talked about is not being talked about.

48. Children begin by loving their parents. After a time, they judge them; rarely is ever do they forgive them.

49. The old believe everything; the middle-aged suspect everything; the young know everything.

50. Nothing succeeds like success.

51. In this world there are only two tragedies – one is not getting what one wants, the other is getting it.

52. To lose one parent may be regarded as a misfortune; to lose both looks like carelessness.

53. To get back one's youth, one merely has to repeat one's follies.

54. Young people nowadays assume that money is everything, and when they get older they know it.

55. It is better to have a permanent income than to be fascinating.

56. No man is ever rich enough to buy back his past.

57. A man cannot be too careful in his choice of enemies.

58. Every great man nowadays has his disciples, but it is always Judas who writes the biography.

59. I have very simple tastes, I am always satisfied with the very best.

60. I like talking to a brick wall, I find it is the only thing that never contradicts me.

61. Whenever people agree with me, I always feel I must be wrong.

62. One half of the world does not believe in God, and the other half does not believe in me.

63. Praise makes me humble, but when I am abused, I know I have touched the stars.

64. I shall have to die, as I have lived beyond my means.

65. To regain my youth, I would do anything in the world, except take exercise, get up early, or become respectable.

66. If this is the way Queen Victoria treats her prisoners, she doesn't deserve to have any.

67. I shall never make a new friend in life, though I rather hope to make a few in death.

68. I have had my hand on the moon; what is the use of trying to rise a little way from the ground?

69. This wallpaper will be the death of me; one of us will have to go.

William Shakespeare

1. Love all, trust a few. Do wrong to none.

2. It is not in the stars to hold our destiny but in ourselves.

3. We know what we are, but know not what we may be.

(Work : Hamlet)

4. Cry "Havoc," and let slip the dogs of war.

(Work : Julius Caesar)

5. I come to bury Caesar, not to praise him.

   The evil that men do lives after them;

   The good is oft interred with their bones."

(Work : Julius Caesar, Act 3, Scene 2)

6. Truth is truth, to the end of reckoning.

7. The valiant never taste of death but once.

Of all the wonders that I yet have heard,

It seems to me most strange that men should fear;

Seeing that death, a necessary end,

Will come when it will come.   *(Work : Julius Caesar)*

8. Cowards die many times before their deaths.

9. Mine honour is my life; both grow in one; take honour from me and my life is done.

10. Friendship is constant in all other things

Save in the office and affairs of love:

Therefore all hearts in love use their own tongues;

Let every eye negotiate for itself

And trust no agent.   *(Work : Much Ado about Nothing)*

11. Suspicion always haunts the guilty mind.

12. So may he rest, his faults lie gently on him!

13. This royal throne of kings, this sceptred isle,

This earth of majesty, this seat of Mars,

This other Eden, demi-paradise,

This fortress built by Nature for herself

Against infection and the hand of war,

This happy breed of men, this little world,

This precious stone set in the silver sea,

Which serves it in the office of a wall

Or as a moat defensive to a house,

Against the envy of less happier lands, —

This blessed plot, this earth, this realm, this England.

(Work : King Richard II)

14. The fool doth think he is wise, but the wise man knows himself to be a fool.

15. And to those thorns that in her bosom lodge,
To prick and sting her.   *(Work : Hamlet)*

16. I feel within me a peace above all earthly dignities, a still and quiet conscience.

17. He wears his faith but as the fashion of his hat.

18. I pray thee cease thy counsel,
Which falls into mine ears as profitless as water in a sieve.

19. And since you know you cannot see yourself, so well as by reflection, I, your glass, will modestly discover to yourself, that of yourself which you yet know not of.

20. I hate ingratitude more in a man
than lying, vainness, babbling, drunkenness,
or any taint of vice whose strong corruption
inhabits our frail blood.

21. It is a wise father that knows his own child.

22. His life was gentle; and the elements
So mixed in him, that Nature might stand up,
And say to all the world, THIS WAS A MAN!

23. See first that the design is wise and just: that ascertained, pursue it resolutely; do not for one repulse forego the purpose that you resolved to effect.

24. Be great in act, as you have been in thought.

25. Strong reasons make strong actions.

26. When we are born, we cry, that we are come to this great stage of fools.

27. Our remedies oft in ourselves do lie.

28. God bless thee; and put meekness in thy mind, love, charity, obedience, and true duty!

29. He who has injured thee was either stronger or weaker than thee. If weaker, spare him; if stronger, spare thyself.

30. If all the year were playing holidays,
To sport would be as tedious as to work.

(Work : King Henry IV)

31. Let me not to the marriage of true minds Admit impediments: love is not love Which alters when it alteration finds.

32. Be not afraid of greatness.

33. So full of artless jealousy is guilt,
It spills itself in fearing to be spilt.   *(Work: Hamlet)*

34. Hereafter, in a better world than this,
I shall desire more love and knowledge of you.
(Work: As You Like It)

35. Love looks not with the eyes, but with the mind.

36. There is a tide in the affairs of men
Which taken at the flood, leads on to fortune;
Omitted, all the voyage of their life
Is bound in shallows and in miseries.   *(Work: Julius Caesar)*

37. A wretched soul, bruised with adversity,
We bid be quiet when we hear it cry;
But were we burdened with like weight of pain,
As much or more we should ourselves complain.

38. It is a wise father that knows his own child.

39. Assume a virtue, if you have it not.

40. The devil can cite scripture for his purpose.
(Work: The Merchant of Venice)

41. Frailty, thy name is woman!

42. Virtue and genuine graces in themselves speak what no words
can utter.

43. The lady doth protest too much, methinks.

44. When griping grief the heart doth wound, and doleful dumps
the mind oppresses, then music, with her silver sound, with
speedy help doth lend redress.

45. But love is blind, and lovers cannot see the pretty follies that
themselves commit.

46. Excellent wretch! Perdition catch my soul,
But I do love thee! and when I love thee not,
Chaos is come again.   *(Work: Othello)*

47. Neither a borrower nor a lender be;
For loan oft loses both itself and friend,
And borrowing dulls the edge of husbandry.
This above all.

48. Our doubts are traitors,
And make us lose the good we oft might win
By fearing to attempt. *(Work: Measure for Measure)*

49. In time we hate that which we often fear.

50. Some rise by sin, and some by virtue fall.

51. The attempt and not the deed confounds us.
(Work: Macbeth)

52. Lord, what fools these mortals be!

53. Ill deeds are doubled with an evil word.

54. While thou livest, keep a good tongue in thy head.

55. How poor are they who have not patience! What wound did ever heal but by degrees?

56. Pray you now, forget and forgive.

57. I understand a fury in your words,
But not the words. *(Work: Othello)*

58. This England never did, nor never shall,
Lie at the proud foot of a conqueror. *(Work: King John)*

59. Age cannot wither her, nor custom stale
Her infinite variety. *(Work: Antony and Cleopatra)*

60. The fashion wears out more apparel than the man.

61. In a false quarrel, there is no true valour.

62. A very ancient and fish-like smell. *(Work: The Tempest)*

63. Conversation should be pleasant without scurrility, witty without affectation, free without indecency, learned without conceitedness, novel without falsehood.

64. The trust I have is in mine innocence, and therefore am I bold and resolute.

65. Your face is a book, where men may read strange matters.

66. What a deformed thief this fashion is.

67. He hath eaten me out of house and home.

68. Oh, that way madness lies; let me shun that.

69. The peace of heaven is theirs that lift their swords, in such a just and charitable war.

70. Life is as tedious as a twice-told tale
Vexing the dull ear of a drowsy man. *(Work: King John)*

71. O, how this spring of love resembleth
The uncertain glory of an April day!
(Work: The Two Gentlemen of Verona)

72. Nothing emboldens sin so much as mercy.

73. Sweet are the uses of adversity, which, like a toad, though ugly and venomous, wears yet a precious jewel in its head.

74. But, for my own part, it was Greek to me.
(Work: Julius Caesar)

75. There are more things in heaven and earth, Horatio,
Than are dreamt of in your philosophy. *(Work: Hamlet)*

76. This is the short and the long of it.
(Work: The Merry Wives of Windsor)

77. How use doth breed a habit in a man!
(Work: The Two Gentlemen of Verona)

78. The hand that hath made you fair hath made you good.
(Work: Measure for Measure)

79. True is it that we have seen better days.
(Work: As You Like It)

80. It is not enough to help the feeble up, but to support him after.

81. Thou shalt be both the plaintiff and the judge of thine own cause.

82. Glory is like a circle in the water,
Which never ceaseth to enlarge itself,
Till by broad spreading it disperses to naught.

83. We have some salt of our youth in us.
(Work: The Merry Wives of Windsor)

84. Life is as tedious as a twice-told tale, Vexing the dull ear of a drowsy man.

85. I wasted time, and now doth time waste me.

86. Misery acquaints a man with strange bedfellows.
(Work: The Tempest)

87. Although the last, not least. *(Work: King Lear)*

88. Truth is truth
To the end of reckoning. *(Work : Measure for Measure)*

89. Good night, good night! parting is such sweet sorrow,
That I shall say good night till it be morrow.

(Work : Romeo and Juliet)

90. The end crowns all,
And that old common arbitrator, Time,
Will one day end it. *(Work : Troilus and Cressida)*

91. The soul of this man is in his clothes.

92. Nothing will come of nothing. *(Work : King Lear)*

93. Full fathom five thy father lies;

94. Of his bones are coral made;
Those are pearls that were his eyes:
Nothing of him that doth fade
But doth suffer a sea-change
Into something rich and strange. *(Work : The Tempest)*

95. But love is blind and lovers cannot see
The pretty follies that themselves commit;
For if they could, Cupid himself would blush
To see me thus transformed to a boy.

(Work : The Merchant of Venice)

96. There is nothing either good or bad, but thinking makes it so.

97. For they are yet ear-kissing arguments.

98. The gods are just, and of our pleasant vices
Make instruments to plague us. *(Work : King Lear)*

99. My words fly up, my thoughts remain below.

100. Is this a dagger which I see before me,
The handle toward my hand? Come, let me clutch thee.
I have thee not, and yet I see thee still.
Art thou not, fatal vision, sensible
To feeling as to sight? or art thou but
A dagger of the mind, a false creation,
Proceeding from the heat-oppressed brain? *(Work : Macbeth)*

101. There are occasions and causes why and wherefore in all
things. *(Work : King Henry)*

102. Like as the waves make towards the pebbled shore, So do our minutes hasten to their end.

103. Now cracks a noble heart. Good night sweet prince.

104. Every man has his fault, and honesty is his.

(Work : Timon of Athens)

105. They say, best men are moulded out of faults,
And, for the most, become much more the better
For being a little bad.   *(Work : Measure for Measure)*

106. Rich gifts wax poor when givers prove unkind.

(Work : Hamlet)

107. Pity is the virture of the law, and none but tyrants use it cruelly.

108. My salad days,
When I was green in judgment.   *(Work : Antony and Cleopatra)*

109. I thank God I am as honest as any man living, that is an old man and no honester than I.   *(Work : Much Ado about Nothing)*

110. Though I am not naturally honest, I am so sometimes by chance.

111. Et tu, Brute!   *(Work : Julius Caesar)*

112. Silence is the perfectest herald of joy: I were but little happy, if I could say how much.   *(Work : Much Ado about Nothing)*

113. I will be correspondent to command, And do my spiriting gently.   *(Work : The Tempest)*

114. Lady you berefit me of all words,
Only my blood speaks to you in my veins,
And there is such confusion in my powers.

115. Our bodies are our gardens to which our wills are gardeners.

116. For Brutus is an honourable man;
So are they all, all honourable men.   *(Work : Julius Caesar)*

117. From the still-vexed Bermoothes.   *(Work : The Tempest)*

118. That man that hath a tongue, I say, is no man,
If with his tongue he cannot win a woman.

(Work : The Two Gentlemen of Verona)

119. Now would I give a thousand furlongs of sea for an acre of barren ground.   *(Work : The Tempest)*

120. Like one
     Who having into truth, by telling of it,
     Made such a sinner of his memory,
     To credit his own lie.   (*Work: The Tempest*)

121. I am not bound to please thee with my answers.

122. When he is best, he is a little worse than a man; and when he
     is worst, he is little better than a beast.
                                      (*Work: The Merchant of Venice*)

123. How many ages hence
     Shall this our lofty scene be acted over
     In states unborn and accents yet unknown!
                                          (*Work: Julius Caesar*)

124. The law hath not been dead, though it hath slept.
                                    (*Work: Measure for Measure*)

125. Speak to me as to thy thinkings,
     As thou dost ruminate, and give thy worst of thoughts
     The worst of words.   (*Work: Othello*)

126. But, soft! what light through yonder window breaks?
     It is the east, and Juliet is the sun.   (*Work: Romeo and Juliet*)

127. Merrily, merrily shall I live now,
     Under the blossom that hangs on the bough.
                                          (*Work: The Tempest*)

128. He is winding the watch of his wit; by and by it will strike.

129. Their understanding
     Begins to swell and the approaching tide
     Will shortly fill the reasonable shores
     That now lie foul and muddy.

130. I have not slept one wink.   (*Work: Cymbeline*)

131. Something is rotten in the state of Denmark.   (*Work: Hamlet*)

132. Home-keeping youth have ever homely wits.
                              (*Work: The Two Gentlemen of Verona*)

133. It is a familiar beast to man, and signifies love.
                              (*Work: The Merry Wives of Windsor*)

134. I, thus neglecting worldly ends, all dedicated
     To closeness and the bettering of my mind.
                                          (*Work: The Tempest*)

135. My library
Was dukedom large enough. *(Work: The Tempest)*

136. I must be cruel only to be kind;
Thus bad begins, and worse remains behind.

137. I wish you well and so I take my leave,
I Pray you know me when we meet again.

138. Praising what is lost makes the remembrance dear.

139. Thy words, I grant are bigger, for I wear not, my dagger in my mouth.

140. By the pricking of my thumbs,
Something wicked this way comes.
Open, locks,
Whoever knocks! *(Work: Macbeth)*

141. I am not merry; but I do beguile
The thing I am, by seeming otherwise. *(Work: Othello)*

142. Your hearts are mighty, your skins are whole.
(Work: The Merry Wives of Windsor)

143. If this were played upon a stage now, I could condemn it as an improbable fiction. *(Work: Twelfth Night)*

144. I have heard of your paintings too, well enough; God has given you one face, and you make yourselves another.
(Work: Hamlet)

145. We do not keep the outward form of order, where there is deep disorder in the mind.

146. Be thou as chaste as ice, as pure as snow, thou shalt not escape calumny. Get thee to a nunnery, go. *(Work: Hamlet)*

147. If there be no great love in the beginning, yet heaven may decrease it upon better acquaintance, when we are married and have more occasion to know one another.

148. I would fain die a dry death. *(Work: The Tempest)*

149. The little foolery that wise men have makes a great show.
(Work: As You Like It)

150. Small cheer and great welcome makes a merry feast.
(Work: The Comedy of Errors)

151. Thou art the Mars of malcontents.
(Work: The Merry Wives of Windsor)

152. I cannot tell what the dickens his name is.

(Work: The Merry Wives of Windsor)

153. My meaning in saying he is a good man, is to have you understand me that he is sufficient.

(Work: The Merchant of Venice)

154. Fill all thy bones with aches. *(Work: The Tempest)*

155. Come not within the measure of my wrath.

(Work: The Two Gentlemen of Verona)

A little more than kin, and less than kind. *(Work: Hamlet)*

156. Double, double toil and trouble;
Fire burn, and cauldron bubble. *(Work: Macbeth)*

157. I will make a Star-chamber matter of it.

(Work: The Merry Wives of Windsor)

158. Cursed be he that moves my bones.

(Work: Epitaph on his gravestone)

159. I pray you bear me henceforth from the noise and rumour of the field, where I may think the remnant of my thoughts in peace, and part of this body and my soul with contemplation and devout desires.

160. O Romeo, Romeo! wherefore art thou Romeo?

(Work: Romeo and Juliet)

161. You cram these words into mine ears against the stomach of my sense.

162. The game is up. *(Work: Cymbeline)*

163. Small to greater matters must give way.

(Work: Antony and Cleopatra)

164. He was a man, take him for all in all,
I shall not look upon his like again. *(Work: Hamlet)*

165. And many strokes, though with a little axe,
Hew down and fell the hardest-timbered oak.

(Work: King Henry VI)

166. A horse! a horse! my kingdom for a horse!

(Work: King Richard III)

167. I will wear my heart upon my sleeve
For daws to peck at. *(Work: Othello)*

168. But to my mind, though I am native here
And to the manner born, it is a custom
More honoured in the breach than the observance.

(Work : Hamlet)

169. Brevity is the soul of wit.   *(Work : Hamlet)*

170. Uneasy lies the head that wears a crown.

(Work : King Henry IV)

171. This is the third time; I hope good luck lies in odd numbers....
There is divinity in odd numbers, either in nativity, chance, or
death.   *(Work : The Merry Wives of Windsor)*

172. What seest thou else
In the dark backward and abysm of time?

(Work : The Tempest)

173. To have seen what I have seen, see what I see!

(Work : Hamlet)

George Bernard Shaw

1. The only service a friend can really render is to keep up your
courage by holding up to you a mirror in which you can see a
noble image of yourself.

2. The man with a toothache thinks everyone happy whose teeth
are sound. The poverty-stricken man makes the same mistake
about the rich man.

3. This is the true joy in life, the being used for a purpose
recognized by yourself as a mighty one; the being thoroughly
worn out before you are thrown on the scrap heap; the being
a force of Nature instead of a feverish selfish little clod of
ailments and grievances complaining that the world will not
devote itself to making you happy.

(Work : Man and Superman, Epistle Dedicatory)

4. Hatred is the coward's revenge for being intimidated.

5. It is a curious sensation: the sort of pain that goes mercifully
beyond our powers of feeling. When your heart is broken,
your boats are burned: nothing matters any more. It is the end
of happiness and the beginning of peace.

6. People are always blaming their circumstances for what they are. I don't believe in circumstances. The people who get on in this world are the people who get up and look for the circumstances they want, and, if they can't find them, make them.

7. I am a Millionaire. That is my religion.   *(Work : Major Barbara)*

8. The people who get on in this world are the people who get up and look for the circumstances they want and if they can't find them, make them.

9. You are going to let the fear of poverty govern your life and your reward will be that you will eat, but you will not live.

10. Power is the faculty or capacity to act, the strength and potency to accomplish something. It is the vital energy to make choices and decisions. It also includes the capacity to overcome deeply embedded habits and to cultivate higher, more effective ones.

11. Censorship ends in logical completeness when nobody is allowed to read any books except the books that nobody reads.

12. Some look at things that are, and ask why. I dream of things that never were and ask why not?

13. Youth, which is forgiven everything, forgives itself nothing: age, which forgives itself everything, is forgiven nothing.

(Work : Man and Superman)

14. Success does not consist in never making mistakes but in never making the same one a second time.

15. People, who say it cannot be done, should not interrupt those who are doing it.

16. Life isn't about finding yourself. Life is about creating yourself.

17. A Native American Elder once described his own inner struggles in this manner: Inside of me there are two dogs. One of the dogs is mean and evil. The other dog is good. The mean dog fights the good dog all the time. When asked which dog wins, he reflected for a moment and replied, "the one I feed the most."

18. She had lost the art of conversation but not, unfortunately, the power of speech.

19. When a stupid man is doing something he is ashamed of, he always declares that it is his duty.

20. A happy family is but an earlier heaven.

21. The more things a man is ashamed of, the more respectable he is. *(Work : Man and Superman)*

22. Never waste jealousy on a real man: it is the imaginary man that supplants us all in the long run.

23. Do not waste your time on Social Questions. What is the matter with the poor is Poverty; what is the matter with the rich is Uselessness.

24. Power does not corrupt men; fools, however, if they get into a position of power, corrupt power.

25. Life is no brief candle to me. It is a sort of splendid torch which I have got a hold of for the moment, and I want to make it burn as brightly as possible before handing it onto future generations.

26. Do you think that the things people make fools of themselves about are any less real and true than the things they behave sensibly about? They are more true: they are the only things that are true. *(Work : Candida)*

27. Beware of the man who does not return your blow: he neither forgives you nor allows you to forgive yourself.

28. Youth is a wonderful thing. What a crime to waste it on children.

29. We are made wise not by the recollection of our past, but by the responsibility for our future.

30. If you have an apple and I have an apple and we exchange these apples then you and I will still each have one apple. But if you have an idea and I have an idea and we exchange these ideas, then each of us will have two ideas.

31. Parentage is a very important profession, but no test of fitness for it is ever imposed in the interest of the children.

32. We are all dependent on one another, every soul of us on earth.

33. Miracles, in the sense of phenomena we cannot explain, surround us on every hand: life itself is the miracle of miracles.

34. Money is the most important thing in the world. It represents health, strength, honour, generosity and beauty as conspicuously as the want of it represents illness, weakness, disgrace, meanness and ugliness.

35. If history repeats itself, and the unexpected always happens, how incapable must Man be of learning from experience.

36. There are two tragedies in life. One is to lose your heart's desire. The other is to gain it.

37. Give a man health and a course to steer, and he'll never stop to trouble about whether he's happy or not.

38. Choose silence of all virtues, for by it you hear other men's imperfections, and conceal your own.

39. No diet will remove all the fat from your body because the brain is entirely fat. Without a brain, you might look good, but all you could do is run for public office.

40. England and America are two countries separated by the same language.

41. The American Constitution, one of the few modern political documents drawn up by men who were forced by the sternest circumstances to think out what they really had to face, instead of chopping logic in a university classroom.

42. The worst sin toward our fellow creatures is not to hate them, but to be indifferent to them: that's the essence of inhumanity.

43. The liar's punishment is not in the least that he is not believed, but that he cannot believe anyone else.

44. If you must hold yourself up to your children as an object lesson, hold yourself up as a warning and not as an example.

45. Perhaps the greatest social service that can be rendered by anybody to the country and to mankind is to bring up a family.

46. When I was young, I observed that nine out of ten things I did were failures. So I did ten times more work.

47. The moment we want to believe something, we suddenly see all the arguments for it, and become blind to the arguments against it.

48. A fool's brain digests philosophy into folly, science into superstition, and art into pedantry. Hence University education.

49. What we call education and culture is for the most part nothing but the substitution of reading for experience, of literature for life, of the obsolete fictitious for the contemporary real.

50. Man gives every reason for his conduct save one, every excuse for his crimes save one, every plea for his safety save one; and that one is his cowardice.

51. I dread success. To have succeeded is to have finished one's business on earth, like the male spider, who is killed by the female the moment he has succeeded in his courtship. I like a state of continual becoming, with a goal in front and not behind.

52. Disobedience, the rarest and most courageous of the virtues, is seldom distinguished from neglect, the laziest and commonest of the vices.

53. Clever and attractive women do not want to vote; they are willing to let men govern as long as they govern men.

54. If parents would only realize how they bore their children! Let them do their duties too.

55. I am of the opinion that my life belongs to the whole community and as long as I live, it is my privilege to do for it whatever I can. I want to be thoroughly used up when I die, for the harder I work the more I live.

56. First love is only a little foolishness and a lot of curiosity.

57. Never fret for an only son, the idea of failure will never occur to him.

58. Reading made Don Quixote a gentleman. Believing what he read made him mad.

59. "Do you know what a pessimist is?" "A man who thinks everybody is as nasty as himself, and hates them for it."

(Work : An Unsocial Socialist)

60. Very few people can afford to be poor.

61. He knows nothing; and he thinks he knows everything. That points clearly to a political career. *(Work : Major Barbara)*

62. Reasonable people adapt themselves to the world. Unreasonable people attempt to adapt the world to themselves. All progress, therefore, depends on unreasonable people.

63. When the military man approaches, the world locks up its spoons and packs off its womankind.

64. The love of economy is the root of all virtue.

65. The fact that a believer is happier than a skeptic is no more to the point than the fact than a drunken man is happier than a sober one.

66. All censorships exist to prevent any one from challenging current conceptions and existing institutions. All progress is initiated by challenging current conceptions, and executed by supplanting existing institutions. Consequently the first condition of progress is the removal of censorships.

67. When a man says money can do anything, that settles it: he hasn't got any.

68. The only way to avoid being miserable is not to have enough leisure to wonder whether you are happy or not.

69. We have no more right to consume happiness without producing it than to consume wealth without producing it.
(Work : Candida)

70. Liberty means responsibility. That is why most men dread it.
(Work : Man and Superman)

71. Peace is not only better than war, but infinitely more arduous.

72. New opinions often appear first as jokes and fancies, then as blasphemies and treason, then as questions open to discussion, and finally as established truths.

73. Life levels all men. Death reveals the eminent.

74. Marriage is an alliance entered into by a man who can't sleep with the window shut, and a woman who can't sleep with the window open.

75. Cruelty must be whitewashed by a moral excuse, and pretense of reluctance.

76. When a man wants to murder a tiger, he calls it sport; when the tiger wants to murder him, he calls it ferocity. The distinction between crime and justice is no greater.

77. Hell is full of musical amateurs.

78. Beware of false knowledge; it is more dangerous than ignorance.

79. Political necessities sometime turn out to be political mistakes.

80. Go on writing plays, my boy, One of these days one of these London producers will go into his office and say to his secretary, "Is there a play from Shaw this morning?" and when she says, "No," he will say, "Well, then we'll have to start on the rubbish." And that's your chance, my boy.

81. Democracy is a form of government that substitutes election by the incompetent many for appointment by the corrupt few.

82. Dying is a troublesome business: there is pain to be suffered, and it wrings one's heart; but death is a splendid thing - a warfare accomplished, a beginning all over again, a triumph. You can always see that in their faces.

83. Beauty is a short-lived tyranny.

84. He who can, does. He who cannot, teaches.
(Work : Man and Superman)

85. We learn from experience that men never learn anything from experience.

86. Hegel was right when he said that we learn from history that man can never learn anything from history.

87. There is only one religion, though there are a hundred versions of it. *(Work : Plays Pleasant and Unpleasant)*

88. Capitalism has destroyed our belief in any effective power but that of self interest backed by force.

89. England and America are two countries separated by a common language.

90. The trouble with her is that she lacks the power of conversation but not the power of speech.

91. It is dangerous to be sincere unless you are also stupid.

92. The golden rule is that there are no golden rules.

(Work : Man and Superman)

93. There is no love sincerer than the love of food.

(Work : Man and Superman)

94. I don't believe in circumstances. The people, who get on in this world, are the people who get up and look for the circumstances they want, and if they can't find them, make them.

95. The minority is sometimes right; the majority always wrong.

96. Statistics show that of those who contract the habit of eating, very few survive.

97. He who has never hoped can never despair.

(Work : Caesar and Cleopatra)

98. The test of a man or woman's breeding is how they behave in a quarrel.

99. Man can climb to the highest summits, but he cannot dwell there long.

100. The secret of being miserable is to have leisure to bother about whether you are happy or not. The cure for it is occupation.

Mao Tse Tung

1. Politics is war without bloodshed while war is politics with bloodshed.

2. Revolution is not a dinner party, not an essay, nor a painting, nor a piece of embroidery; it cannot be advanced softly, gradually, carefully, considerately, respectfully, politely, plainly and modestly. Every Communist must grasp the truth: "Political power grows out of the barrel of a gun.

3. Once all struggle is grasped, miracles are possible.

4. I voted for you during your last election.

5. We shall heal our wounds, collect our dead and continue fighting.

6. Communism is not love. Communism is a hammer which we use to crush the enemy.

7. The enemy advances, we retreat; the enemy camps, we harass; the enemy tires, we attack; the enemy retreats, we pursue.

8. The guerilla must move amongst the people as a fish swims in the sea.

9. The cardinal responsibility of leadership is to identify the dominant contradiction at each point of the historical process and to work out a central line to resolve it.

10. War can only be abolished through war, and in order to get rid of the gun, it is necessary to take up the gun.

11. Learn from the masses, and then teach them.

12. In time of difficulties, we must not lose sight of our achievements.

13. Weapons are an important factor in war, but not the decisive one; it is man and not materials that counts.

14. Genuine equality between the sexes can only be realized in the process of the socialist transformation of society as a whole.

15. Enable every woman who can work to take her place on the labour front, under the principle of equal pay for equal work.

16. The people, and the people alone, are the motive force in the making of world history.

17. Khrushchev should get a one-ton medal.

18. If you want to know the taste of a pear, you must change the pear by eating it yourself. If you want to know the theory and methods of revolution, you must take part in revolution. All genuine knowledge originates in direct experience.

19. Letting a hundred flowers blossom and a hundred schools of thought contend is the policy for promoting progress in the arts and sciences and a flourishing socialist culture in our land.

20. Our attitude towards ourselves should be "to be satiable in learning" and towards others "to be tireless in teaching."

21. Political work is the life-blood of all economic work.

22. The differences between friends cannot but reinforce their friendship.

23. Let a hundred flowers bloom, let a hundred schools of thought contend.

24. Take the ideas of the masses (scattered and unsystematic ideas) and concentrate them (through study turn them into concentrated and systematic ideas), then go to the masses and propagate and explain these ideas until the masses embrace them as their own.

25. The atom bomb is a paper tiger which the United States reactionaries use to scare people. It looks terrible, but in fact it isn't... All reactionaries are paper tigers.

26. Women hold up half the sky.

27. In waking a tiger, use a long stick.

28. A revolution is not a dinner party, or writing an essay, or painting a picture, or doing embroidery.

29. The world is yours, as well as ours, but in the last analysis, it is yours. You young people, full of vigour and vitality, are in the bloom of life, like the sun at eight or nine in the morning. Our hope is placed on you.

30. Political power grows out of the barrel of a gun.

31. There is a serious tendency toward capitalism among the well-to-do peasants.

32. There is in fact no such thing as art for art's sake, art that stands above classes, art that is detached from or independent of politics. Proletarian literature and art are part of the whole proletarian revolutionary cause.

33. Passivity is fatal to us. Our goal is to make the enemy passive.

34. In general, any form of exercise, if pursued continuously, will help train us in perseverance. Long-distance running is particularly good training in perseverance.

35. When the enemy advances, withdraw; when he stops, harass; when he tires, strike; when he retreats, pursue.

36. People like me sound like a lot of big cannons.

37. Politics is war without bloodshed, while war is politics with bloodshed.

38. Investigation may be likened to the long months of pregnancy, and solving a problem to the day of birth. To investigate a problem is, indeed, to solve it.

39. Let one thousand flowers bloom.

40. All reactionaries are paper tigers.

41. Despise the enemy strategically, but take him seriously tactically.

42. We think too small, like the frog at the bottom of the well. He thinks the sky is only as big as the top of the well. If he surfaced, he would have an entirely different view.

43. Swollen in head, weak in legs, sharp in tongue but empty in belly.

Mahatma Mohandas Gandhi

1. An eye for an eye makes the whole world blind.

2. Whatever you do will be insignificant, but it is very important that you do it.

3. Always aim at complete harmony of thought and word and deed. Always aim at purifying your thoughts and everything will be well.

4. The weak can never forgive. Forgiveness is the attribute of the strong.

5. Happiness is when what you think, what you say, and what you do are in harmony.

6. What difference does it make to the dead, the orphans and the homeless, whether the mad destruction is wrought under the name of totalitarianism or the holy name of liberty or democracy?

7. Honest differences are often a healthy sign of progress.

8. Unity to be real must stand the severest strain without breaking.

9. It is better to be violent, if there is violence in our hearts, than to put on the cloak of non-violence to cover impotence.

10. Freedom is not worth having if it does not include the freedom to make mistakes.

11. They can not take away our self respect if we do not give it to them.

12. The weak can never forgive. Forgiveness is the attribute of the strong.

13. Honest disagreement is often a good sign of progress.

14. I want freedom for the full expression on my personality.

15. Indolence is a delightful but distressing state; we must be doing something to be happy.

16. In the attitude of silence the soul finds the path in an clearer light, and what is elusive and deceptive resolves itself into crystal clearness. Our life is a long and arduous quest after Truth.

17. I think it would be a good idea.

(Work : when asked what he thought of Western civilization)

18. You must not lose faith in humanity. Humanity is an ocean; if a few drops of the ocean are dirty, the ocean does not become dirty.

19. As long as you derive inner help and comfort from anything, keep it.

20. One needs to be slow to form convictions, but once formed, they must be defended against the heaviest odds.

21. I believe in equality for everyone, except reporters and photographers.

22. Let no one say that he is a follower of Gandhi. It is enough that I should be my own follower. I know what an inadequate follower I am of myself, for I cannot live up to the convictions I stand for. You are no followers but fellow students, fellow pilgrims, fellow seekers, fellow workers.

23. I may live without air and water, but not without Him. You may pluck out my eyes, but that cannot kill me. You may chop off my nose but that will not kill me. But blast my belief in God, and I am dead.

24. Live as if you were to die tomorrow. Learn as if you were to live forever.

25. Be the change that you want to see in the world.

26. Those who say religion has nothing to do with politics do not know what religion is.

27. Courage has never been known to be a matter of muscle; it is a matter of the heart. The toughest muscle has been known to tremble before an imaginary fear. It was the heart that set the muscle trembling.

28. Between husband and wife there should be no secrets from one another. I have a very high opinion of the marriage tie. I hold that husband and wife merge in each other. They are one in two or two in one.

29. Even if you are a minority of one, the truth is the truth.

30. I like your Christ, I do not like your Christians. Your Christians are so unlike your Christ.

31. Where there is love there is life.

32. Every moment of your life is infinitely creative and the universe is endlessly bountiful. Just put forth a clear enough request, and everything your heart desires must come to you.

33. Manliness consists not in bluff, bravado or lordliness. It consists in daring to do the right and facing consequences whether it is in matters social, political or other. It consists in deeds, not in words.

34. What do I think of Western civilization? I think it would be a very good idea.

35. Better far than cowardice is killing and being killed in battle.

36. Don't listen to friends when the Friend inside you says 'Do this.'

37. If we are to teach real peace in this world, and if we are to carry on a real war against war, we shall have to begin with the children.

38. Man can never be a woman's equal in the spirit of selfless service with which nature has endowed her.

39. Manliness consists in making circumstances subserve to ourselves.

40. Non-violence and cowardice go ill together. I can imagine a fully armed man to be at heart a coward. Possession of arms implies an element of fear, if not cowardice. But true non-violence is an impossibility without the possession of unadulterated fearlessness.

41. Non-violence is the greatest force at the disposal of mankind. It is mightier than the mightiest weapon of destruction devised by the ingenuity of man.

42. Power is of two kinds. One is obtained by the fear of punishment and the other by acts of love. Power based on love is a thousand times more effective and permanent then the one derived from fear of punishment.

43. Suffering cheerfully endured, ceases to be suffering and is transmuted into an ineffable joy.

44. The badge of the violent is his weapon, spear, sword or rifle. God is the shield of the non-violent.

45. The hardest metal yields to sufficient heat. Even so must the hardest heart melt before sufficiency of the heat of non-violence. And there is no limit to the capacity of non-violence to generate heat.

46. Suffering has its well-defined limits. Suffering can be both wise and unwise, and when the limit is reached, to prolong it would be not unwise but the height of folly.

47. Non-violence and truth are inseparable and presuppose one another.

48. Man falls from the pursuit of the ideal of plain living and high thinking the moment he wants to multiply his daily wants. Man's happiness really lies in contentment.

49. I suppose leadership at one time meant muscles; but today it means getting along with people.

50. A nation's culture resides in the hearts and in the soul of its people.

51. I have found by experience that man makes his plans to be often upset by God, but, at the same time, where the ultimate goal is the search of truth, no matter how a man's plans are frustrated, the issue is never injurious and often better then anticipated

52. Hatred ever kills, love never dies such is the vast difference between the two. What is obtained by love is retained for all time. What is obtained by hatred proves a burden in reality for it increases hatred.

53. I believe in the fundamental truth of all great religions of the world.

54. It is unwise to be too sure of one's own wisdom. It is healthy to be reminded that the strongest might weaken and the wisest might err.

55. The difference between what we do and what we are capable of doing would suffice to solve most of the world's problem.

56. The moment there is suspicion about a person's motives, everything he does becomes tainted.

57. Prayer is a confession of one's own unworthiness and weakness.

58. Morality is the basis of things and truth is the substance of all morality.

59. Man becomes great exactly in the degree in which he works for the welfare of his fellow-men.

60. Interdependence is and ought to be as much the ideal of man as self-sufficiency. Man is a social being.

61. Among the many misdeeds of the British rule in India, history will look upon the act depriving a whole nation of arms as the blackest.

62. Human kind has to get out of violence only through non-violence. Hatred can be overcome only by love. Counter-hatred only increases the surface as well as the depth of hatred.

63. I am prepared to die, but there is no cause for which I am prepared to kill.

64. Humility cannot be an observance by itself. For, it does not lend itself to being deliberately practised. It is, however, an indispensable test of 'Ahimsa.' For one who has 'Ahimsa' in him it becomes part of his very nature.

65. The first condition of humaneness is a little humility and a little diffidence about the correctness of one's conduct and a little receptiveness.

66. I claim to be an average man of less than average ability. I have not the shadow of a doubt that any man or woman can achieve what I have, if he or she would make the same effort and cultivate the same hope and faith.

67. Intolerance betrays want of faith in one's cause.

68. Is it not enough to know the evil to shun it? If not, we should be sincere enough to admit that we love evil too well to give it up.

69. It is any day better to stand erect with a broken and bandaged head than to crawl on one's belly, in order to be able to save one's head.

70. It is my own firm belief that the strength of the soul grows in proportion as you subdue the flesh.

71. Surely conversion is a matter between man and his Maker who alone knows his creatures' hearts. A conversion without a clean heart is, in my opinion, a denial of God and Religion. Conversion without cleanliness of heart can only be a matter of sorrow, not joy, to a godly person.

72. Restraint never ruins one's health. What ruins it, is not restraint but outward suppression. A really self-restrained person grows every day from strength to strength and from peace to more peace. The very first step in self-restraint is the restraint of thoughts.

73. Non-cooperation with evil is as much a duty as is cooperation with good.

74. Must I do all the evil I can before I learn to shun it? Is it not enough to know the evil to shun it? If not, we should be sincere enough to admit that we love evil too well to give it up.

75. Men often become what they believe themselves to be. If I believe I cannot do something, it makes me incapable of doing it. But when I believe I can, then I acquire the ability to do it even if I didn't have it in the beginning.

76. Let everyone try and find that as a result of daily prayer he adds something new to his life, something with which nothing can be compared.

77. It is through truth non-violence that I can have some glimpse of God. Truth non-violence are my God. They are the obverse and reverse of the same coin.

78. It is man's social nature which distinguishes him from the brute creation. If it is his privilege to be independent, it is equally his duty to be inter-dependent. Only an arrogant man will claim to be independent of everybody else and be self-contained.

79. I will far rather see the race of man extinct than that we should become less than beasts by making the noblest of God's creation, woman, the object of our lust.

80. Have I not gazed at the marvellous mystery of the starry vault, hardly ever tiring of the great panorama?

81. God forbid that India should ever take to industrialism after the manner of the west... keeping the world in chains. If our nation took to similar economic exploitation, it would strip the world bare like locusts.

82. Everyone has faith in God though everyone does not know it. For everyone has faith in himself and that multiplied to the nth degree is God. The sum total of all that lives is God. We may not be God, but we are of God, even as a little drop of water is of the ocean.

83. Destruction is not the law of humans. Man lives freely only by his readiness to die, if need be, at the hands of his brother, never by killing him. Every murder or other injury, no matter for what cause, committed or inflicted on another is a crime against humanity.

84. A certain degree of physical harmony and comfort is necessary, but above a certain level it becomes a hindrance instead of a help. Therefore, the ideal of creating an unlimited number of wants and satisfying them seems to be a delusion and a snare.

85. It is easy enough to be friendly to one's friends. But to befriend the one who regards himself as your enemy is the quintessence of true religion. The other is mere business.

86. I will far rather see the race of man extinct than that we should become less than beasts by making the noblest of God's creation, woman, the object of our lust.

87. Where love is, there God is also.

88. We must become the change we want to see in the world.

89. Anger and intolerance are the enemies of correct understanding.

90. Are creeds such simple things like the clothes which a man can change at will and put on at will? Creeds are such for which people live for ages and ages.

91. As human beings, our greatness lies not so much in being able to remake the world - that is the myth of the atomic age - as in being able to remake ourselves.

92. Democracy must in essence, therefore, mean the art and science of mobilising the entire physical, economic and spiritual resources of all the various sections of the people in the service of the common good of all.

93. Each one prays to God according to his own light.

94. Everyone who wills can hear the inner voice. It is within everyone.

95. Experience convinces me that permanent good can never be the outcome of untruth and violence. Even if my belief is a fond delusion, it will be admitted that it is a fascinating delusion.

96. Faith... must be enforced by reason... when faith becomes blind it dies.

97. Fear has its use but cowardice has none.

98. First they ignore you, then they laugh at you, then they fight you, then you win.

99. Freedom is never dear at any price. It is the breath of life. What would a man not pay for living ?

www.ingramcontent.com/pod-product-compliance
Lightning Source LLC
LaVergne TN
LVHW020048160726
843469LV00043B/1561